AF316677

Jessica Tucker

SET APART

Experiencing Freedom Through the Daniel Fast

Set Apart: Experiencing Freedom Through The Daniel Fast

Clear Wind Publishing

Rights Department, P.O. Box 8344, Jackson, WY 83002

Library of Congress Cataloging-in-Publication Data is available.

ISBN: 9798218120016

PRAYER OF DEDICATION

For my Father and my Friend,

You are worthy to be exalted.

I pray that You are pleased,

Lifted up,

Magnified.

Please take this offering and divide it up

Specifically to each person who reads it

In the way that only You can.

We long to know You, Lord.

Be glorified, My King.

Amen.

TABLE OF CONTENTS

Part 1:

THE DANIEL FAST

Part 2:

DEVOTIONALS

Part One:

THE DANIEL FAST

Introduction

There are assignments I have been tasked to do in my life for which I felt prepared. Some of those tasks coincided with a course of study I had completed, a field of work in which I had experience, or a topic I had researched for several years.

Then there was the assignment of writing this book.

They say that He does not call the qualified; He qualifies the called. I used to regard that statement as a cliché. Now, it's an anchor in my spirit. I am no clergy member, theologian, or preacher. I have no formal education in the Scriptures. I have never been a seminary student. I even spent ten years out of church. I am just a woman who loves Jesus; and that was enough for Him. God called me to write this book for you and for me. It is His heart to draw us closer to Him because He knows that is the safest place we could ever be.

My prayer is that this book will be a tool you can use to guide you in the practice of fasting—specifically, the Daniel Fast. I pray your journey will lead you to greater love for and intimacy with the Lord. I pray your desire for Him increases to be greater than any other desire you have for anything or anyone else. I trust He will respond to your obedience in fasting by speaking to you, healing you, and transforming you.

> **CONSECRATION IS THE SETTING APART OF ONESELF.**

Daniel provides for us an example of consecration—the setting apart of oneself. We can use this example in the Scriptures to guide us how to do the same in our personal walk with God. His obedience, courage, and discipline is a picture of a heart yielded to God and a person who wants to express their love of God through action.

A submitted heart leads to a submitted life.

As you embark on your journey with the Daniel Fast, write down your experiences. Our memories can sometimes fail us. When we need to be reminded of His goodness, of His providence, of His protection, we can look back to what we wrote and know that He is, indeed, still good.

THE HEART OF THE MATTER

Fasting is a beautiful journey with the Lord that has been a blessing to many people. Please do not allow the Enemy to cause you to feel any shame or condemnation if you have a health condition that prevents you from fasting. I urge you to consult with your medical provider prior to beginning any type of fast for the first time.

Some health conditions limit the option of fasting or for how long a person can fast. For example, if you have a predisposition to disordered eating, diagnosed or not, fasting may not be for you at this time. That does not mean God is any less pleased with you. He loves you. He sent His Son as the divine action of His love for you. He is not waiting around for you to earn that love. It is free if you will accept it.

> ## GOD LONGS FOR YOU TO BE NEAR TO HIM.

Only participate in the fast if it is Spirit-led, confirmed by your medical provider, and will not serve as a stumbling block physically, spiritually, mentally, or emotionally. God longs for you to be near to Him. He approves you because He sees you through the Blood of Jesus. Because of that, you are already enough.

THE BEGINNING OF THE JOURNEY

One year in December, God gave me a word as I was preparing for my day. He told me to tithe and fast. This seemed like an unhelpful answer to my prayers that God would give me direction for my life. My fleshly pride peeked out as I thought, "I do tithe. And certainly, God isn't asking *me* to fast." After all, He knew how physically active I was and how many daily calories I "needed" to sustain my life. I laughed a little internally, but He persisted. I had never successfully fasted with water only for more than a day, and I had never even attempted the Daniel Fast.

He took me to a sermon series on tithing that I saw in my YouTube feed previously but never watched. I didn't understand what I could possibly get from the sermon series because I already tithed (or so I thought). The pastor in one of the sermons made a very simple statement: "To tithe is to return the first fruit of all your increase to the storehouse." The Holy Spirit illuminated that statement right then and said to me, "You do not tithe from all your increase. You only tithe from one income stream."

The weight of that statement nearly dropped me to the floor. I had to hold on to the table that I wanted to hide under for support. He was right. God had blessed me with several income streams, and it never occurred to me to tithe from each one of them. It annihilated my fleshly pride that had peeked out earlier. I felt ashamed of my display of ungratefulness. But God, my Redeemer, said, "Now that you are aware, begin tithing correctly as you are learning in this sermon series." I vowed to do so from that day forward. He followed, "And while you're at it, start the Daniel Fast on January 1st."

One

HE CHOSE ME

The instruction to begin the Daniel Fast was daunting to say the least. I even half-jokingly, half-seriously asked God if I could tithe double instead of fasting. I'm not sure if I waited for an answer to that since I knew what it would be. God wanted a deeper level of obedience from me and homed in on two critical areas to develop me—dependence on Him and going to Him first for comfort.

The tendency toward independence and the internal locus of control from which I operate is not necessarily negative or sinful. I believe my responsibilities are my own, I should work for what I want, and I am not owed anything. It is wise to be very discerning in choosing those people with whom we will be interdependent. It is good stewardship to do the best we can with what God has allowed us to have. However, the problem arises when these issues affect my relationship with God. Sure, there are some people I cannot trust, and with whom I should set firm boundaries. I should not be pushing off my responsibilities onto others, either. I should be an enterprising and accomplished person to the best of my ability. But I cannot be so focused on producing and achieving that I block the Holy Spirit from showing me His glory. There are many things I used to strive and struggle to do by myself that I found out later I should have just let God do it.

> # BRINGING GOD GLORY IS MUCH MORE IMPORTANT THAN PERSONAL ACHIEVEMENT.

He is better than me at everything! And if I will just listen to Him, He will guide me in the parts He wants me to do, where He wants me to participate, and the obedience He desires of me. He wanted me to put my full weight on Him. I hadn't been doing that. I was just kind of leaning on Him a little. Every time I think about it now, lines from a hymn called "What a Friend We Have in Jesus" come to mind:

Oh, what peace we often forfeit

Oh, what needless pain we bear

All because we do not carry

Everything to God in prayer! [i]

There was peace He already had for me, solutions He had already worked out, and plans He already formed. But I was committed to doing things myself and therefore missing out on God's hand of intervention.

THE TRUE TITHE

An area where I needed to rely on and submit to the Lord was in my finances. Since God had revealed to me I was not tithing in a complete and biblical way, I researched the meaning of a true tithe. I learned the tithe is a tenth or 10 percent (see Genesis 14:19–20) and that the number 10 is the number of testing. I also learned the tithe must be first (upon receiving any financial increase, the tithe is the first portion to be paid [see Genesis 4:2–5]), it belongs to the Lord (He has reserved that portion for Himself [see Leviticus 27:30]), and expresses my gratitude (all that I have is because of Him, and He meets my every need [see 1 Chronicles 29:13–14]).

Another important lesson I learned was which number to base on the 10 percent. I used to question whether I should tithe from my gross or net income. I wish I could remember which pastor I heard say this. He solved my internal struggle with one simple question, "How much of it do you want God's hand on?" My answer? I want God's hand on everything. I want Him involved in every area of my life. I want to serve Him completely. The answer became so simple, and I chose to tithe 10 percent of the gross amount of all financial increase that entered my life.

By returning the first of my financial increase to the Lord, I communicated I trust Him above trusting that which He gave me. When I was only tithing from one income source, not tithing from my gross income, and not tithing in a timely manner, I was communicating that I must manage my own finances for there to be enough, and that God could not be trusted to do that. A true tithe is orderly, timely, and complete. I made a financial plan that reflected obedience in the area of tithing.

A TRUE TITHE IS ORDERLY, TIMELY, AND COMPLETE.

Now, I sometimes wake up in the middle of the night to pay my tithes. I don't say this to toot my own horn. I just want to illustrate how God has shifted my heart toward excitement at the thought of obedience in this area. I am grateful for an opportunity to show Him in a small way that I appreciate Him and the sacrifice of His Son on the cross.

Prior to starting this journey, I found so much security in having money. Since security was important to me, He used the topic of money at the start of my Daniel Fast journey to get my attention. Then, over time, He adjusted my heart toward money until I looked up one day and it was not important in the same way anymore. It's not that I no longer cared about money or having it. I do. It is that I came to see Him as my true security; money became one of the many tools He uses to bring me that security. Then I switched my research to the Daniel Fast.

EXPLORING THE DANIEL FAST

The extent of my knowledge of the Daniel Fast was that it involved a biblical term called "pulse." To be obedient to God, I needed to be educated on it quickly. I purchased a book on the Daniel Fast and bookmarked the book of Daniel in my Bible. I began researching using these resources and developed a shopping list. For the first day, I had a plan for how I would prepare and cook my food. This process was a crash course version of approaching the next 21 days of my life.

As I learned about the Daniel Fast, my attitude shifted slowly from complaint to a spiritual curiosity of what God would do during the next three weeks. My desire to obey Him superseded my desire for my favorite foods. I realized that food had become a space of idolatry and that gluttony had crept into my spirit.

When I felt stressed or overwhelmed, I ate. When I needed guidance or was confused, I ate. When I was excited about something or had an accomplishment, I ate. I loved food. It was where I went first. I allowed the excuse that I exercised regularly to hide the spirit of excess that was within me. I included God in the little piece of a prayer I would do before a meal, but I was not honoring Him the way He deserves. I went to food before I went to God, and that made it an idol.

An unfortunate but common behavior among believers is the tendency to pick the "bad sins" and focus on those while giving themselves a free pass on the "small sins." Sin is sin. Before my first Daniel Fast, I arrogantly questioned God by asking, "Lord it's just food. It's not like I'm out here doing drugs, sleeping around, getting drunk… Can't I just have food?"

I repeated similar sentiments to my best friend on the phone one day, and he said, "Oh, so you think that just because your vice is food, God doesn't want to take away that idol too?"

> # ANYTHING WE GO TO BEFORE GOD IS AN IDOL.

It was a humbling but necessary thing for him to say. He was right. By going to food for comfort before going to God, I had made an idol out of it. Further, I was committing gluttony. I made the excuse for a long time that I could eat what I wanted as long as I exercised and maintained a certain level of fitness. But the gluttony was in the excess. Just because it may not have produced certain undesirable outcomes in my body does not mean my heart was not out of order. I was overindulgent, and I was overeating. God wanted to deliver me from that. My prolonged overindulgence could have easily turned into a binge eating disorder. I'm grateful that God redirected me before that became the case.

As I researched the Daniel Fast, I picked out a few recipes that I would try—secretly hoping I could make every one of them taste like the food I normally ate. I also purchased a new journal and wrote in it some things I wanted to talk with the Lord about, areas I wanted Him to move in, and situations where I needed guidance.

In the days leading up to the fast, I tried to shift my perspective on some things. One concern I had was that by completing the Daniel Fast I would lose too much weight. That probably sounds weird to some people; but my reasoning is that I find value in being a certain size, so I am able to perform certain tasks that require strength. The way I shifted my perspective on my concern about losing too much weight was that I would likely not be tempted to treat the Daniel Fast as a diet plan.

Another concern I had was that I would not have adequate energy to get through my days, which were often demanding. I shifted my thoughts: Maybe I will have more energy since I will eat more nutritious foods.

I was concerned that the category of food I would miss the most might cause me to stumble during the fast—sugar. Going without meat or deep-fried foods or any drinks that were not water? No problem. But sugar? I actually asked the Lord, "How?"

I committed to trusting and obeying the Lord in this. I had my Daniel Fast book and Bible passages prepared as a guide, I had my pantry and refrigerator filled with ingredients I would need, and I had my first day of meals cooked the night before. I was ready.

GETTING STARTED

The first three days of the fast felt like torture, and often I cried over my meals. At night, I had hot flashes and sweating spells. I was very fatigued and almost felt depressed. At one point, I almost went to the emergency room because I felt so sick. But I knew the likely response I would get, after some questions from the doctors, would be to just stop fasting. I remember thinking that I must have been eating so poorly before, but did not realize the extent. That my body was responding this way to healthy foods was concerning.

But something wonderful happened when I woke up on the fourth morning. I felt like a superhero. I was energized, excited about the day, and ready to face whatever was before me. My mind was clear. My emotions were at peace. And I was most of all eager to hear from God.

ON YOUR BEHALF

When the Holy Spirit directed me to fast, He also changed a goal I had for my upcoming birthday on March 9th. I planned to pay off a certain debt of mine as a birthday gift to myself. However, the Holy Spirit said not to pay that debt, but to set aside $10,000 to pay the remainder of a debt my sister owed. I was more than happy to do that for her, but there was only one problem. I didn't have $10,000.

I thought that maybe by some miracle, from January 1st to March 9th, I could come up with the money. I wanted to be obedient, so my first instinct was to find ways to work and earn extra money to do this. The Holy Spirit told me to just follow Him. By the end of January, not only did I not have a dime to set aside for my sister, but I barely had any savings. Financial issue after issue had come up and drained it. I was at nearly nothing altogether. Completely uncomfortable, I felt like I was failing my sister. She is one of the hardest working people I have ever met. I knew God was doing this for her to acknowledge her heart for Him and to show her that she is His daughter; and He can give her any good gift He wants. But there I was with my savings drained.

One revelation the Lord gave me during my fast was to never again borrow money for any reason. So, I was not to borrow to achieve this either. On February 8th, I had $500 to set aside for my sister's debt. I only had 30 days left to make this happen. But what is time to God?

On March 7th, two days before my birthday, I went to visit my sister and handed her a check for $10,000. Only God can do something like that. He rained it out of the sky in 30 days. He did it that way on purpose, so I would know, she would know, and everyone who would ever hear the story would know that God is Jehovah Jireh. He is the Provider.

This deepened my faith in Him. It also showed my sister that God loves her so much that He would rearrange someone else's life to provide for her. The Holy Spirit was responding to my sister's gratitude and the obedience and discipline she had already exhibited. She had already paid nearly 90 percent of the debt herself. She worked seven days a week tirelessly to take care of her responsibility. The Lord saw. So, he alleviated the last $10,000 because He is kind like that.

> **ONE OF THE NAMES OF GOD IS JEHOVAH JIREH, WHICH MEANS "GOD WILL PROVIDE."**

My sister had no idea the entire time that God was working this on her behalf. She was simply rising each day and choosing to live for and with the Lord. God does not always announce to us the move He is about to make in our lives, but we can rest assured that any move He makes is for our good and His glory.

The Lord gave my sister and me a story that we will never forget—something to lean on when things are murky or unclear or when we are in trouble. He is faithful. So, we never have to be afraid.

THE SHIFT

When God calls you to do something, He will woo your heart and turn your desires toward it—even if you never felt that way before. He just needs obedience. I love to fast now. I no longer think of it as depriving myself. Now, I think of it as taking care of myself spiritually, physically, emotionally, and mentally. I have adopted some tenants of the Daniel Fast even when I'm not fasting, and I feel better than I ever have in my life.

I think He used me on purpose. I thought there was absolutely no way I could ever do any sort of fast from food, and God knew that. I think that part of why He used me is because I was someone who did not think I could ever fast, much less ever enjoy fasting. We see His pattern of using the unqualified and unequipped in Scripture. He used Moses to speak when he had a speech impediment (see Exodus 4:10). He called Jeremiah to be a prophet while he was very young (see Jeremiah 1). He used Gideon to deliver the Israelites from bondage even though he was afraid (see Judges 6). The Lord knew that by using me and shifting my heart, He would get the glory.

Two

DANIEL'S EXAMPLE

The account of the fast performed by Daniel can be found in Daniel chapters 1 and 10. Daniel chapter 1 begins by describing how the king of Babylon, Nebuchadnezzar, besieged Jerusalem while it was under the rule of King Jehoiakim. Nebuchadnezzar wanted young, handsome, wise men of Israel trained to serve him in the palace. Included in their training was consumption of the king's choice food and drink. The sons of Judah chosen for the task were Daniel, who was given the name Belteshazzar by the chief of the king's eunuchs; Hananiah, who was called Shadrach; Mishael, who was called Meshach; and Azariah, who was called Abed-Nego.

Daniel 1:8 says, "But Daniel purposed in his heart that he would not defile himself with the portion of the king's delicacies, nor with the wine which he drank; therefore he requested of the chief of the eunuchs that he might not defile himself" (NKJV).

The Bible says God gave Daniel favor in the eyes of the chief of the eunuchs. The chief was afraid that Daniel's request not to take the king's food and drink would put his life in danger. He was concerned that they would not look as healthy or strong as those who accepted the king's food. Daniel was right to refuse the king's food and drink to be obedient to God. But notice what he did. He was respectful and asked permission for him and his three friends to be tested in the matter. He did not allow the fact that he was right to make him haughty and obstinate.

> **"PULSE" IS FOOD THAT COMES FROM THE GROUND.**

He requested 10 days of eating "pulse" and drinking only water. Pulse is food that comes from the ground—vegetables. Daniel asked that at the end of the 10 days, they be examined and compared to the others. He said to the chief that after the examination, "As you see fit, so deal with your servants" (Daniel 1:13 NKJV). This showed that he trusted God's instructions to him as being perfect. He had no need to prove himself—only to be obedient to God.

When the 10 days ended, Daniel and his three friends were examined; their physical appearances were better than those who consumed the king's food. So, their portion of the king's food was removed from them, and they were given the pulse and water on which they had been tested. God gave the four men knowledge and wisdom; Daniel could interpret dreams and visions.

Then we arrive at the passage that is the anchor Scripture of this book. It is a statement of what God will do when we consecrate ourselves to Him. He sets us apart. He gives us supernatural increase, and He uses us in miraculous ways. Let's read Daniel 1:18–19:

> *18 At the end of the time set by the king to bring them into his service, the chief official presented them to Nebuchadnezzar. 19 The king talked with them, and he found none equal to Daniel, Hananiah, Mishael and Azariah; so they entered the king's service. 20 In every matter of wisdom and understanding about which the king questioned them, he found them ten times better than all the magicians and enchanters in his whole kingdom (NIV).*

"None equal."

The earthly king witnessed what following our heavenly King will do. He saw the benefits of obedience. He witnessed the working of faith. Daniel's example is what we follow in this Daniel Fast journey. We will step out in faith. We will anticipate God's presence, and we will experience a more fruitful life with Him.

GUIDELINES OF FASTING

There are different types of fasts mentioned in the Scriptures. One type of fasting is a partial fast, which is the category the Daniel Fast falls under because food is consumed during the fast—but only certain types. Another type is a water-only fast where no food is eaten and only water is consumed. An example of this is Jesus fasting for 40 days and nights in Matthew 4:2. It is generally accepted that Jesus drank water, but did not eat food because at the end of the fast, the Scriptures say Jesus was "hungry," but thirst is not mentioned.

Next is what is called a total or absolute fast where no food or drink is consumed. There are two 40-day accounts of Moses fasting this way in Exodus 34:28 and Deuteronomy 9:18. The last type of fasting is a supernatural fast—one that supersedes what the natural body can handle. The total fasts performed by Moses were also supernatural or divinely enabled because the human body cannot last that long without food or water.

"FASTING" MEANS TO PUT AWAY FOOD.

Something to consider as you seek the Lord about fasting is its definition and meaning. Fasting is from food, and the term "fasting" means to put away food. Abstaining from other activities can be obedience to God if He has called you to do so, but fasting, in the biblical sense, is only true fasting if you are abstaining from food. There are so many wonderful benefits of fasting such as developing a deeper sense of humility, drawing closer to God, and hearing His voice more clearly.

The length of the Daniel Fast is 10 days or 21 days. Ten days comes from the testing period with Daniel and his friends. A full Daniel Fast is 21 days based upon Daniel 10:2–3: "In those days I, Daniel, was mourning three full weeks. I ate no pleasant food, no meat or wine came into my mouth, nor did I anoint myself at all, till three whole weeks were fulfilled" (NKJV).

The above passage in the book of Daniel also gives us insight into what foods can and cannot be consumed during the Daniel fast. There should be no meat or animal products, which includes eggs, dairy, honey, and seafood. There should also be no "pleasant" foods, which includes sweeteners like sugar, sugar substitutes, syrup, nectar, or chocolate. Foods that also should be avoided are foods that contain additives, have been chemically processed or treated, or that contain preservatives. The only drink to be consumed is water; tea, alcohol, juice, coffee, or caffeinated drinks should not be consumed.

> **FOLLOW THE LORD'S SPECIFIC LEADING OF YOU DURING THE FAST.**

The foods that Daniel did consume are those that come from the ground. Those foods are fruits, vegetables, nuts, seeds, beans, legumes, herbs and spices, and whole grains. Whole grains can be used to make bread, but it must be unleavened (no active yeast). Oils made from vegetables that have not been chemically produced or treated can be used as well as milks made from nuts that have also not been chemically processed. Chapter 5 gives examples of foods that can be eaten on the Daniel fast, as well as a few recipes to help you get started.

Another important note is being open to the Lord's specific leading of you during the fast. The Lord may also ask you to remove a food during the Daniel Fast that is permitted. For example, I love pineapple. I could eat bowls of it. Since I am aware of that, I ask God if there is a "further" for me within the Daniel Fast when I do it.

FIVE TIPS FOR A SUCCESSFUL DANIEL FAST

Preparation is key—especially when we are trying something new. So, we will walk through five tips for a successful fast that you can use on your journey.

1. Ask your doctor for guidance prior to starting your fast—especially if you have a pre-existing health condition.

You will want to ensure you are still following the recommendations of your health care provider while participating in the Daniel Fast. Describe to your doctor the guidelines of the Daniel Fast so they can properly advise you on any adjustments that may need to be made based upon a health condition. Also, be careful and aware of any food allergies or sensitivities you may have. Checking the labels on food items is an important practice for anyone on the Daniel Fast. It is especially important for ensuring you will consume nothing that would be detrimental to your health.

For those who do not have health conditions that could affect their fasting, I do not recommend "editing" the fast. It's an easy thing to do if you feel like the Daniel Fast is drastic. Ask God for clear communication on your body's threshold when you start. You do not want to confuse detox symptoms with actual illness or harm to the body and quit prematurely. I believe God honors our desire to be obedient to Him in the area of fasting and will protect our bodies as we fast. Once you get past the first few days, you will start to experience the benefits of eating highly nutritious, whole foods.

I have witnessed people who have more trouble with the concept of a Daniel Fast than a water fast. I think that some of this can be attributed to the length of the Daniel Fast versus a water-only fast. The human body can only last for days with no food. The Daniel Fast is an extended fast over 21 days. Sometimes, people are tempted to then "edit" the fast to include certain meat or certain sweets, etc. Ask the Lord for His help to do the Daniel Fast accurately and completely, keeping in mind applicable guidance from your doctor.

2. Have accountability partners and involve those who live with you.

If you live with family members or roommates, invite them to participate in the Daniel Fast with you. If you live alone, you can ask a fellow church member, Bible study group member, or a friend to go on the Daniel Fast journey with you. You can participate in the Daniel Fast with a church, but you do not have to only fast when your church does. Ask the Lord to show you who He would like to walk this journey with you. Sometimes, He will ask you to walk the journey alone with Him. It is important to listen to His instruction each time you are about to start a Daniel Fast.

While it is okay to involve others in your fast, we are not called to "announce" our times of fasting to get attention or "credit" from people or from God. No one needs to know you are fasting outside of those who are on the journey with you. The Bible says in Matthew 6:16, "Moreover, when you fast, do not be like the hypocrites, with a sad countenance. For they disfigure their faces that they may appear to men to be fasting. Assuredly, I say to you, they have their reward" (NKJV). Ask the Lord who He wants to walk with you, tell only them, and complete the fast from a place of humility.

3. Practice cooking and incorporating Daniel Fast meals before the fast begins.

This is especially important if this way of preparing food is new to you. During my first Daniel Fast, I thought I would make a dish that involved black beans for Day 1. It's funny now, but it was not funny at the time. The black beans I purchased were dried, not canned. The label said to soak the beans for a long while, but I did not think it could possibly take that long for them to be ready to cook.

Well, I was wrong. When I pulled the beautiful black bean and brown rice stuffed peppers out of the oven and took a bite, I was met with an unappetizing crunch. I was in a full-blown panic. That was all I had to eat! True story, I had to go through each one and pick out every bean and cook them separately again before mixing them back into the peppers. It was still not tasty, but at least the beans were not crunchy.

That leads to another part of the recommendation: Buy enough ingredients for several days at a time, ahead of time. Practice cooking some dishes, and also have a well-stocked pantry and fridge with ingredients you can use if you have a mishap while you are fasting.

Other adjustments to make in the days leading up to your fast is to begin incorporating the Daniel Fast meals you are practicing ahead of the fast, significantly increase your water consumption, taper back foods that are not consistent with the Daniel Fast, remove non-Daniel Fast food from your home, and adjust your exercise regimen as needed while your body adjusts to fasting.

4. Plan for events that involve food and have Daniel Fast snacks with you while you are out and about.

Is there an event that you are scheduled to attend during your fast that will involve food? If yes, then request a menu ahead of time so you can plan what you will eat when you arrive. Often, special requests can be accommodated with enough advanced notice. If there is no way for accommodations to be made that are suitable for the Daniel Fast, check to see if you can reschedule for a time after your fast has ended. Another question to ask is if you can bring your own food with you to the event or establishment.

It is likely that you will experience at least a few times throughout the 21 days when you are away from home and very hungry. Have quick snacks available like a bag of nuts, some fruit, or unleavened bread and natural almond or peanut butter with you so you do not break your fast with unpermitted foods.

5.   Set your intention for the fast while being open to God's direction.

We are fearfully and wonderfully made (Psalm 139:14). Our bodies are the temples where the Holy Spirit chooses to reside, so we ought to treat them well. We honor Him by taking care of our bodies. More than that, we honor Him by stewarding well our spiritual lives. Ask God for His plan for your time of prayer and fasting. Align your intentions with what He tells you. Seeking the heart of God is paramount. He will meet you during your fast to communicate His heart to you.

ENDING THE FAST WELL

End the fast gradually and safely. I do not recommend immediately eating every food you did not have during the Daniel Fast, as soon as the 21 days are over. Reintroduce foods slowly so you do not get sick. Start with light foods and refrain from anything heavy until your body has time to adjust. End the fast much like how you began. Continue with some meals being Daniel Fast meals after the fast has concluded.

Ask the Lord if there are any tenets of the Daniel Fast He would like for you to continue after the fast has ended. These can be physical, like continuing to cut out a certain food, or they can be spiritual, like waking up at a certain time in the morning to spend time with Him. Our times of fasting are special, but they should not be so unique as to have no resemblance to the lives we lead when we are not fasting.

Three

PUT HIM FIRST

The Bible is clear about Who should come first in our lives. In Matthew 22:35–38 (NKJV), a Pharisee asked Jesus, what is the greatest commandment in the law? Jesus answered him that it is to "love the LORD your God with all your heart, with all your soul, and with all your mind. This is the first and great commandment" (NKJV). First is the only place God can be. He knows we need Him to be in that position because there is nothing and no one else who can sustain us the way He does.

One of the wonderful qualities about our Lord is that He does not call us to put Him first as some sort of dictatorship. He calls us into a life-giving relationship with Him. There is no greater pleasure in this life than proximity and deep intimacy with the Lord. In Him is all safety, all provision, all abundance, and the meeting of needs. He gives us all the tools we need to navigate life as a believer. He speaks to us through His excellent Word because He loves us so much. The writer of Psalm 119 discusses the pleasure that comes from meditating on the Word of God in verses 97–104:

97 Oh, how I love Your law!

It is my meditation all the day.

98 You, through Your commandments, make me wiser than my enemies;

For they are ever with me.

99 I have more understanding than all my teachers,

For Your testimonies are my meditation.

100 I understand more than the ancients,

Because I keep Your precepts.

101 I have restrained my feet from every evil way,

That I may keep Your word.

102 I have not departed from Your judgments,

For You Yourself have taught me.

103 How sweet are Your words to my taste,

Sweeter than honey to my mouth!

[104] Through Your precepts I get understanding;

Therefore I hate every false way (NKJV).

THE BENEFITS

Being children of God comes with many benefits. We are not only given the gift of an eternity with Him, but we can also live lives of favor that bring glory to the King and expand His Kingdom. In order for us to live the kind of lives that attract other people to the Lord, we need to be filled to the brim and overflowing with Him. The purpose of this 21-day fast is to consecrate ourselves and draw near to Him so we can do just that—reflect Jesus.

> **SOME OF THE GREATEST PERIODS OF SPIRITUAL CLARITY OCCUR WHILE FASTING.**

Consecration means setting apart for a sacred purpose. When we set ourselves apart, we create the space needed for us to be open and sensitive to the voice of the Lord. Denying our flesh lifts our spirit and clears the way for Him to reign freely in our hearts. It quiets the opposing voices and sharpens our focus on Him. I have found that some of the periods of greatest clarity I have had in my life were during times of fasting.

THE PREEMINENCE OF GOD

More important than getting every step of the fast "right" is allowing God the preeminence that is due Him. He is Premier, and our ability or inability to see Him that way has no bearing on the fact that He is First and Only. When our hearts and lives come into agreement with this, we benefit from participating in divine order. How wonderful is it that the supreme, divine Creator of all things desires to speak with each of us, desires to guide us, and delights in correcting us because He knows what is best for us?

It is important to follow the rules of the fast because it reflects an obedient heart that seeks to subdue the flesh. However, we should not become so preoccupied with each rule and the legalism of them that we are distracted from the heart and purpose of the fast. Our relationship with Him is critical to living the life He has for us that resides under His preferred and perfect will.

I have spoken with people over the years who would say that if they "mess up" during the fast, they might as well end the fast and try again another time. I think a better response to an occurrence such as that is to go to the Lord, repent, and ask for forgiveness. Ask Him to show you what led you to stray from the fast. Ask Him to show you His heart, what He wants you to learn, and how to get back on track. He is a God of grace!

Remember how the Enemy will rationalize and twist the truth to deceive you. I have always found it interesting that Matthew 4:1–11 does not say Jesus was led by the Spirit to the wilderness to fast and then the devil came to tempt Him because he saw Jesus was hungry and vulnerable. No, it states that "Jesus was led up by the Spirit into the wilderness to be tempted by the devil." Notice the word "to". Jesus does fast for 40 days while there in the wilderness, but the primary purpose of His placement in the wilderness was to be tempted by the devil.

Your fasting serves a purpose. Jesus communed with the Spirit for 40 days. So, when Satan came to tempt Him with manipulated versions of the truth, Jesus was able to respond to Satan with absolute truth. James 4:7 says to "resist the devil and he will flee from you" (KJV). Jesus did just that as the devil tempted Him. The devil had to leave Him. And Jesus was ministered to by angels.

> **IF YOU FEEL RESISTANCE DURING YOUR FAST, RESIST BACK.**

If you feel resistance, either internally, from other people or environmentally as you prepare to begin your fast, resist back. The Enemy would love to help you rationalize out of it because he understands the transformative power of the Lord and how God can use a fast to dispense that power.

God certainly does not do everything I want or ask Him to do. But I can say that He always moves during and following a fast. Every time, I feel closer to Him. Every time, more of His nature is revealed to me. Do not let the Enemy or anyone else take that gift from you. God is faithful, and He will respond to your obedience.

TIMING IS IMPORTANT

I like to think of spending time with God before I start my day in the morning as returning to Him the first fruits of my time. It is He who gives me the blessing of time and is so merciful to allow me another day to worship Him. Part of showing gratitude for that is to do nothing else prior to meeting with Him each day.

There was a time, years ago, when I did not commune with God first thing in the morning. I did something else and did not even realize it until He corrected me. There are habits we sometimes have unknowingly. We may wake up and immediately check our phones or browse the web or respond to "just a few emails." For me, the first action of my day reflected a latent trust in the resources God allotted to me over trust in Him as the Source of everything I am.

My devotional time came second. I did not open my eyes and say, "Thank You, Lord, for allowing me to see another day." I did not open my Bible and allow the Lord to illuminate His Word to me in a new way, as He so often does. I did not whisper a prayer of gratitude to the One who saved my life.

Oh no.

I opened my eyes, searched my bed frantically for my phone, and checked every single financial account and property value to ensure it was all still there. It is mortifying to think about now.

The only reason I have the presence of mind to do the work God has called me to do is because He gave me my mind and kept it active and present. The only reason that I took the paths in life I took to get me to a certain place financially is because He guided my steps. The only reason I am even here, alive on this earth, and can generate any income is because He decided to give me another breath.

So, one day, I woke up to do my normal routine of checking my accounts before acknowledging God, and He stopped me in my tracks. He asked me a simple question, "Who gave that to you?"

I set my phone down beside me in my bed. He continued, "Who brought you out of lack into abundance?" I felt my head bow and my shoulders slump. He asked another question, "Who rebuked the devourer for your sake?"

I could have laid on the cold wood floor. He was right. I was allowing the trauma of lack in my past to cause me to make an idol out of the resources He had given me. I was allowing anxiety about ending up back in a previous season to block my trust in God. I repented and asked the Lord to help me keep Him first. He deserves it. And I thanked Him for His correction of me. I was grateful He loved me enough to discipline me.

WE NEED HIS HELP

Jeremiah 17:9 says, "The heart is deceitful above all things, And desperately wicked; Who can know it?" (NKJV). We need the Lord's help to follow His instructions for our lives. Times of prayer and fasting are key to allowing God to mold our hearts into obedient hearts He can use.

I mentioned in Chapter 1 how God used the topic of security and money to get my attention about fasting. He knew that He needed to address the roots of fear I had surrounding that so I would no longer be bound in that area. I wanted to be obedient to God, but I also felt that I had to provide for myself by myself. Sometimes, we project onto God the wounds we have from other people. Since I felt like I could not depend on other people for security, I unknowingly did not allow God to fully provide me the security I needed either.

I placed impossibly high standards of achievement on myself. I defined success using sky-high measurements. I developed a need to perform, accomplish, execute a tiresome list of tasks and goals. I was living with none of the ease God made available to me. He knew that and wanted better for me, so He used the Daniel Fast to expose those tendencies to me.

The areas in which we feel anxiety are easy candidates for those things we can intentionally or unintentionally place before God. We can be concerned about our health, worried about our children, insecure about our finances, or agonizing about the outcome of a situation over which we have no control.

It is good to bring those topics to the Lord during a fast. Our feelings are natural, but they are not God. Sometimes, we feel like we can't stop worrying about something or allowing it to consume our thoughts. And in our own strength, that could be true. So, we must invite Him in. He knew we would need His help to keep His commandments. That is precisely why He sent His Holy Spirit to us. He is our Divine Helper.

When we put God first and heed His Holy Spirit, we receive the advantages of the fruit of His Spirit. Romans 15:13 says it this way: "Now may the God of hope fill you with all joy and peace in believing, that you may abound in hope by the power of the Holy Spirit" (NKJV). Place Him as head of your life and heart and watch Him make miracles on the foundation of your obedience.

YIELDING AND TESTIFYING OF HIS WILL

For years, I was afraid to testify about how God had moved in my life. The fears ranged from concern that people would think I was a terrible person for facing the things I faced to fear that people would hear my stories of overcoming and resent me for them. The Enemy convinced me to tell no one of the experiences I had and how God brought me through. Satan could not take away my obedience to God, but he could silence my testimony so that it could not be used to witness to others. I was deceived into thinking my silence was noble and showed humility.

If I intended to tell my testimony and take the credit for it, that would be extremely problematic. But we are supposed to tell others about the goodness of God. As I studied His Word, I came across this phrase in Revelation 12:11: "And they overcame him by the blood of the Lamb and by the word of their testimony" (NKJV). It's both. It is salvation and testifying.

My first step was recording those things God had done in my life so that over time, as my memories faded, I could go back and read them. I could relive His providence in those moments of recollection and use them to give me peace about the future. Documenting the moves of God shows us just how much we need Him. I could write something every day about Him. During your fast, you may find yourself writing more than usual. Be vigilant because the Enemy desires to interrupt and stop this. He wants you to think you are sufficient by yourself and that you don't need God the way you do.

THE ENEMY OF YOUR LIFE AND YOUR FAST

Lucifer allowed the sin of pride to overcome him and move him to attempt to place himself above or before God. Because of that sin, the Bible says Lucifer fell "like lightning" from heaven (Luke 10:18). He is now the Adversary, the Accuser, the Enemy—Satan. And since he did not succeed in superseding the Most High, he has now made it his mission to separate us from the Lord. He wants to tempt us into sin so that we, too, will succumb to our prideful lusts. He wants to rob as many as he can out of an eternity with the Lord. He wants as much glory for himself as he can acquire.

The Enemy is God's antithesis. God is all truth, light, and love. The Enemy is evil and a liar. In fact, in John 8:44, Jesus speaks of the devil this way:

"You are of your father the devil, and your will is to do your father's desires. He was a murderer from the beginning, and does not stand in the truth, because there is no truth in him. When he lies, he speaks out of his own character, for he is a liar and the father of lies" (ESV).

It's difficult to imagine pure evil. Often, when we think of someone as a "bad person," we still may think there is at least a little bit of good in them. For the Enemy, that is simply not so. It is critical to view the Enemy correctly, so we are not deceived. He is a liar. Everything he says is a lie. He is not capable of speaking the truth. There is no goodness, no decency, no mercy present in him. So, as you fast and as you walk through this life, understand that there is a real adversary working hard against you.

> **THE ENEMY IS WORKING HARD AGAINST YOU; BUT, HE IS DEFEATED.**

But the devil is defeated!

Our All-Powerful God has already won. It is our job to walk in that victory and give the devil no room in our hearts and lives. The good news is that God truly keeps us from being consumed. He has new mercy every morning, and He does not run out. We can find strength in waiting on Him. He has given us the practice of fasting as a gift. It is a time for us to draw near to Him, derive strength from Him, and focus our hearts on Him. The closer we find ourselves to the King, the less we desire to do that which does not please Him. And the deeper we love Him, the more we want to tell the world of His goodness.

LISTENING FOR HIS VOICE

We have all heard some version of the adage: "If you want something you've never had, you must do something you've never done." I made it a very serious part of my life to research and study the topic of hearing the voice of God. I would follow instructions in the books I read and model the example of pastors and teachers in the faith whom I respected. These were all very helpful. But there was a depth—a level of intimacy that came when I denied my flesh and fasted.

Prioritize spending time with Him every day. I remember missing one morning of devotional time during my first Daniel Fast. As the day progressed, I felt ill in a way that I could not explain. I was tired, nauseous, and melancholy. I prayed and asked God why I felt so downcast when I had been feeling so wonderful throughout most of the fast. He told me I had not spent time with Him yet that day. At that moment, I realized how much more important spiritual food is than physical food. I immediately opened the Word and talked with God. I felt replenished right away.

> **THE DANIEL FAST IS NOT A DIET PLAN. IT IS A TIME OF CONSECRATION WITH OUR SAVIOR.**

Nothing else mattered outside of Him. This was proof that the Daniel Fast is not some diet plan, although there are physical benefits to completing it. Rather, it is a time of spiritual consecration and communion with our Savior. Denying the flesh meant that I could clearly hear Him. It meant that I was sensitive to His voice. It meant that I anticipated hearing from Him. It also sent me into a place where my faith was cultivated. Instead of coming before the Lord timidly just hoping He might speak, I went before Him boldly, anticipating and expecting that He would speak.

I'll admit, I haven't spent much time in the parts of the Bible that are lists of generations or the portions that give details and measurements about how things were to be built. But one day, I realized I was missing critical Bible passages. During the Daniel Fast, I came across Exodus chapter 25. The Lord was giving instructions on how He wanted the Israelites to give offerings in the sanctuary, and how the Ark of the Testimony, the Table for the Showbread, and the Gold Lampstand were to be fashioned.

The Lord gave explicit details in His instructions to include measurements, materials, and procedures. As I read, the Holy Spirit reminded me of a prayer time I had with Him previously. In that prayer time, He took me back to Anatomy and Physiology class. He reminded me of when I was studying microsurgery on the hand. It fascinated me how finely tuned and precise the instruments must be to complete such a surgery. The accuracy the surgeon must have to direct the instruments to such tiny parts was astonishing, and I thought how powerful it was that the nervous system and muscular system are all intertwined and designed so marvelously.

The Holy Spirit told me I needed to be so in tune with Him that He can touch the finest, smallest part of me and move my whole being. He said I should be so close to Him that I could hear a whisper. He wanted to be able to give me the kind of instructions He gave in Exodus and know that I was close enough to hear them and follow them exactly. I was to become so familiar with Him that I recognized His voice in all different environments. As I repeated the Daniel Fast over the years, the Lord used those times to sharpen my ability to hear Him.

REPEATING THE DANIEL FAST

During my first Daniel Fast, I felt like signs from God were overt and clear. I would pray and ask God to speak or move in a certain area and often received confirmation in apparent ways. Many times along the way, God reassured me that I was on the path He had set. As I repeated the Daniel Fast and deepened in my walk with Him over time, those signs became less overt. It is not that the Holy Spirit does not want to speak with me now. Rather, it is that as I come to know His heart on a deeper level, I no longer need such overt signs. As I mature in Him, I can handle a more advanced relationship with Him.

> **GOD IS UNCHANGING; BUT HE CANNOT BE RELEGATED TO AN EQUATION.**

For the first few years I completed the Daniel Fast, I followed a pattern of twice a year in the same months each year. Those were the times I felt He was leading me to fast. One year, He changed the pattern by changing one of the months that He called me to fast. God is immutable, which means that He is unchanging. But that does not mean He can be relegated to an equation. It does not mean He will always follow that same pattern. It is important to be yielded to Him in a way that you are mature enough spiritually for Him to change the method by which He accomplishes a thing through you and still get your obedience.

Each time I completed the Daniel Fast was a unique and special experience. I look forward to those times now because I know that not a moment of it will be wasted. He will make the best use out of it all. He often uses the Daniel Fast to guide me into and out of seasons, to answer a petition or request that I have for Him, and to develop me to be able to be used in a deeper way spiritually. I am always changed, always renewed, and always filled at the end of each Daniel Fast.

WE MUST TESTIFY

We serve a great God. He heals us, sustains us, keeps us, delivers us, and saves us, and we ought to be grateful to Him for it. We ought to express our gratitude by thanking Him directly and witnessing to others about His redemptive power. The Bible says in Psalm 107:1–2, "Oh, give thanks to the Lord, for He is good! For His mercy endures forever. Let the redeemed of the Lord say so, Whom He has redeemed from the hand of the enemy" (NKJV).

We are the redeemed of the Lord. We should *say so*.

Do not allow the Enemy to deceive you into silence about your testimony. Allow the Holy Spirit to guide you, instead of fear or anxiety. God has given you a specific assignment, a unique calling, and a distinct purpose. Satan would love for you to believe the lie that your testimony is not significant or helpful. That way he can keep those who are meant to hear your testimony from experiencing the fullness of God. We must remain focused on the things the Lord says about us and resist the Enemy and his lies.

When the Lord moves you to speak, then speak. When He says to declare His goodness, declare it. When He says to give your testimony, testify. We don't know who needs to hear our story to encourage them. We cannot fathom how God can choose to express His love for an individual through the words we say. We have no idea whose life and eternity would be shifted as we speak.

We must speak. We must declare. We must testify.

Five

BREAD OF LIFE

Chapter 2 contains a quick story about my attempt to make stuffed peppers during my first Daniel Fast. Here's the thing: I had not made stuffed peppers ever before. I don't know that it would have been successful even outside of the Daniel Fast. While fasting will challenge you and push you outside of your comfort zone (both of which are healthy and necessary for growth), it is wise to begin the journey with some elements that will make it easier to stay on track. By learning to adapt foods I already loved to the Daniel Fast, I took away any excuses that I could have conjured up that would have ended my fast prematurely.

As you continue on your journey, there is so much creativity to be used and fun to be had during the fast. Once you have set a foundation, you may find yourself excited about trying new recipes and cooking in ways that you have not before. Eventually, the line between how you eat while you are fasting and how you eat while you are not may be blurred into being barely distinguishable.

There were times when I was on the Daniel Fast that I was in a place of desperation. I had pleaded with God to intervene in someone's life. Other times, healing was needed. Yet other times, clarity that only God could give was needed. During these times, it is very helpful to have staple foods that you can make with little effort so that you have the emotional, spiritual, and physical bandwidth to endure a spiritual battle. The Lord is your strength, so ultimately that comes from Him. But reducing areas of stress can help us be ready to receive what we need from the Lord.

I used to unknowingly subscribe to the mindset that if I was doing something "for God," it had to be prohibitively difficult. I had this subconscious idea that if the process wasn't painstaking or grueling, it wasn't holy. I know now that is untrue. I remember when I began enjoying being on the Daniel Fast. This fear crept up in me that I was not adequately fasting because I was no longer suffering to do it. In my mind, it was wonderful that I enjoyed spending time with God; but it somehow was not right that I was beginning to also enjoy the physical part of the fast.

> **COMING TO ENJOY A SPIRITUAL DISCIPLINE IS A POSITIVE THING.**

The Holy Spirit debunked that myth. It is not a negative thing to come to enjoy fasting. The Bible talks about how God loves a cheerful giver (see 2 Corinthians 9:7). For some, giving is strenuous at first; they later look forward to doing so and actively search for opportunities to obey God in that way. Part of walking with God is growing in affection toward the things of God. He used fasting to eradicate my "no pain, no gain" mentality, which was closely related to my tendency to strive and work in my own strength. When I allowed God to be Father and Lord, rest entered my life. I am so much better now because of it.

So, do not allow the Enemy to trick you into feeling guilty about incorporating elements that make fasting easier. Spending time with the Lord is the goal. The things we do to assist with that will help keep our eyes on what matters most. When we begin our obedience to the Lord in a certain area, it may be difficult. We find comfort in what the Bible says in Hebrews 12:11: "No discipline seems pleasant at the time, but painful. Later on, however, it produces a harvest of righteousness and peace for those who have been trained by it" (NIV).

START WITH WHAT YOU KNOW

The first time I completed the Daniel Fast was also the first time in my life that I would be cooking exclusively foods that come from the ground. I already did not enjoy cooking (although I love to eat), so I was nervous about taking on the task. An approach that I realized later that would have been helpful initially would be to take my favorite recipes and dishes and adapt them to the Daniel Fast. For example, one of my favorite dishes when I was growing up was turkey meatloaf, mashed potatoes, and green beans. I still feel a smile in my stomach when I think about it. The approach to recreating this meal the Daniel Fast way would be to look at the ingredients and swap the ones out that do not belong.

For the green beans, instead of butter, use olive oil. For broth, use homemade vegetable broth. Onions, garlic, spices, and herbs can all be used in the fast, so the rest is easy. Then, there are the mashed potatoes. Instead of cow's milk, use a nut milk like almond milk. No butter can be used; but with some good seasoning, you won't miss it. Finally, there is the meatloaf. You may think like I used to, that there is no way to have a good substitute for that dish. I learned quickly that a delicious Daniel Fast "meatloaf" can be made by substituting chickpeas for the meat. A flour like almond, oat, or whole wheat flour or ground flaxseed is good for holding the loaf together. Again, for milk, almond milk instead of cow's milk can be used. Dicing up sweet and savory vegetables like carrots, celery, garlic, and onion gives it flavor; and being generous with a seasoning blend is key. A food

> **A GREAT TIP FOR A DANIEL FAST RECIPE IS TO MODIFY YOUR FAVORITE DISH.**

processor can be used to combine the chickpeas, vegetables, flour or flaxseed, milk, and seasonings to form into a loaf. I use tomato paste to top the loaf, and it tastes great!

Maybe you are already vegetarian or vegan. If that is the case, you will likely have less to substitute in your recipes. Be sure to check the ingredients for processing, additives, or chemical by-products that are not permitted. Those who are vegan or vegetarian are likely already aware of good sources of protein to consume while on the Daniel Fast. Soybean foods like tofu or tempeh are great sources of protein that are also versatile. Other sources of proteins are beans, lentils, brown rice, quinoa, nuts, and seeds. Consuming adequate protein will help your body to function properly and optimally, especially for individuals who are highly physically active.

A DAY IN THE LIFE

Let's walk through a day of meals for the Daniel Fast. I like to start the day with a glass of water before breakfast. The first meal of the day can be a bowl of oatmeal topped with fruit, a bowl of sprouted whole grain cereal with nut milk, scrambled tofu and vegetables, or a fruit and vegetable smoothie. To add variety to oatmeal, add chia seeds or sliced almonds and vary the fruit toppings. To whole grain cereal, add cinnamon or nut butter with blueberries and bananas. Scrambled tofu is delicious with onions, garlic, and your favorite seasonings. Pure fruit juices with no added sugar or extra ingredients can be used to make smoothies along with nut milks.

Sandwiches are a popular lunch choice. So, during the fast, an option to try is a bean burger with a side of roasted potatoes, salad, and sliced avocado. I like using black beans to make burgers. Sautéing onions, garlic, and peppers in olive oil to be combined in a food processor with black beans, rolled oats, and seasonings makes a delicious mixture for the patties. The patties can be cooked on the stovetop in some olive oil or baked in the oven. A simple unleavened bread can be made by forming a dough with whole wheat flour, olive oil, and a little salt. The bread will be flat because there is no yeast or rising agent. Top the burger with your favorite vegetables, and season with pure tomato paste for a dressing. Potatoes can be sliced into wedges and roasted as a side dish. A simple salad dressing can be made with olive oil, lemon juice, and herbs. Slice some avocado to complete your lunch plate.

Some dinner options are brown rice and beans, lentil and potato soup, or vegetable chili. Rice and beans is a repeated dinner dish for me as it is delicious, filling, and a great source of protein. For many dinner dishes, I used a slow cooker so that each day there is a great meal prepared by the evening. Maybe your family has a recipe they have passed down or you have a favorite in a cookbook. Check the ingredients, substitute as necessary, and prepare enough for leftovers.

Throughout the day, some great snacks are nuts, raisins, fruits, vegetables, crackers and natural almond or peanut butter, or hummus. Stay away from foods that are indulgent during the fast—particularly those foods that would distract you from the focus and point of the fast, which is seeking God. When I am fasting, a dessert I like is "ice cream," made by chopping and freezing fruit and then blending it with coconut milk. However, if I feel led to avoid desserts altogether, I do not prepare it.

YOUR GROCERY LIST

Sometimes when people think of fasting, they frame it based on the list of foods they cannot have. Part of coming to love fasting was to focus more on the list of foods that I could eat, which were both nutritious for my body and delicious. Chapter 2 lists the guidelines of fasting and the foods that are and are not permitted in the fast. Those foods are any animal products, dairy, artificial sweeteners, any beverages that are not water, and any foods that are processed, refined, or do not come from the ground. The foods that are permitted on the fast are abundant. Below are some examples of foods you can incorporate during the Daniel Fast:

Beans and Legumes: Black Beans, Black-Eyed Peas, Chickpeas, Kidney Beans, Lentils, Navy Beans, Peanuts, Pinto Beans, Soybeans

Beverages: Water

Fruits: Apples, Avocados, Bananas, Blueberries, Cranberries, Grapes, Oranges, Kiwis, Lemons, Limes, Peaches, Pears, Strawberries, Tomatoes, Watermelons

Herbs and Spices: Basil, Black Pepper, Cilantro, Cinnamon, Cumin, Curry, Dill, Nutmeg, Oregano, Paprika, Parsley, Rosemary, Sage, Salt, Thyme, Turmeric

Milk: Almond Milk, Cashew Milk, Coconut Milk

Nuts: Almonds, Cashews, Pecans, Pistachios, Walnuts

Oils: Avocado Oil, Coconut Oil, Olive Oil, Sesame Oil

Seeds: Chia Seeds, Flaxseeds, Pumpkin Seeds, Sunflower Seeds

Vegetables: Asparagus, Broccoli, Cabbage, Cauliflower, Celery, Cucumber, Garlic, Ginger, Kale, Onion, Potato, Spinach, Sweet Potato, Zucchini

Whole Grains: Barley, Brown Rice, Millet, Oats, Quinoa, Whole Wheat

This list is not exhaustive but is meant to give you a starting point as you begin shopping for ingredients. There are certain categories where anything of that type is permitted. Those categories are beans and lentils, fruits, herbs and spices, nuts, vegetables, and whole grains.

RECIPES

If you are anything like me, you like some guidance and structure when starting something new. I asked a very gifted friend to create a day's worth of Daniel Fast recipes—breakfast, lunch, dinner, a snack, and a smoothie—so that we have some ideas on where to begin while planning to cook and prepare food for the fast. First is a recipe for overnight oats for breakfast:

Fig and Raspberry Overnight Oats

½ cup unsweetened coconut milk

½ cup fresh raspberries

2 figs, cut in half

1 inch of vanilla bean

2 teaspoons fresh squeezed lemon juice

a pinch of salt

Blend all of these ingredients.

In a separate bowl:

2 cups of whole grain oats

1 tablespoon chia seeds

½ teaspoon cinnamon

Add the blended mixture to the oats and mix well. Transfer to a couple of mason jars and let sit in the fridge for at least 6 hours (overnight). Enjoy in the morning!

Next is a salad for lunch that is very simple but delicious. All ingredients are common in grocery stores. To prepare the ingredients that are to be shaved or thinly sliced, you can use a mandolin to make the shaving and slicing more uniform, but it can certainly be done with a knife.

Cabbage Salad

1 small purple cabbage, shaved or very thinly sliced

1 fennel bulb, shaved or very thinly sliced

1 Granny Smith apple, sliced thinly

1 carrot, shredded

Rinse and drain all ingredients; set aside in a large bowl together.

For the vinaigrette:

1½ cups extra virgin olive oil

the juice of one lemon

4–5 sprigs of cilantro

salt and pepper to taste

Add ingredients into a blender and blend until smooth. Coat salad with the vinaigrette and enjoy.

For dinner is a spaghetti squash with sauce that is also hearty and easy to make. The recipe calls for nutritional yeast, which is an inactive yeast that gives the flavor of cheese. If you are not comfortable using that ingredient or feel led to not use it, please omit it.

Spaghetti Squash

Preheat oven to 350 degrees

1 spaghetti squash, rinsed well, cut in half (lengthwise), and seeds removed

1 tablespoon avocado oil

2 sprigs of sage

2 sprigs of thyme

salt and pepper to taste

Rub the inside of the squash with the oil: 1–1½ teaspoons on each half should be plenty. Lightly salt. Add one sprig of sage and thyme to each half. On a baking pan, place the squash so that the seasoned side is facing down in the pan (herbs should be under each half). Roast in the oven until tender. Depending on the size, it should take 35–45 minutes.

For the sauce:

2 large tomatoes, cored

2 cloves garlic

½ red onion, diced (about ½ cup)

¼ cup fresh basil

A few tablespoons of avocado oil or extra virgin olive oil

2 tablespoons of nutritional yeast (optional)

Blend ingredients in blender and set aside.

Once squash is done and cool enough to handle, scoop out the "noodles" and place in a bowl. Mix in sauce to your liking. You can serve in individual bowls or place back into the squash shell and use that as your bowl.

Pico de Gallo is a tasty snack that you can make in batches and refrigerate to have other servings later.

Pico de Gallo

4 Roma tomatoes, diced

1 small onion, diced

1 jalapeño, seeded and diced (removing the seeds takes away most of the heat)

½ cup fresh pineapple, diced

juice of ½ lime

¼ cup extra virgin olive oil or avocado oil

a few sprigs of cilantro, diced

salt and pepper to taste

Mix all of the ingredients together and refrigerate for about an hour.

This is delicious on some crispy pieces of romaine lettuce. Or you can try the chip recipe below, if your fast allows.

Whole Wheat Tortilla Chips

whole wheat tortillas, cut into quarters

a drizzle of avocado oil

a pinch of salt

Lightly brush the tortillas with a little oil and a pinch of salt. Bake in oven at 350° until crispy (usually about 10 minutes).

Finally, we have a green smoothie that can be prepared as a breakfast or snack option throughout your day.

Delicious Green Smoothie

6 ounces fresh spinach

2 cups fresh pineapple

2 apples, cored and quartered

2 radishes

1 celery rib

½ cucumber

½ cup sunflower seeds (no shell)

½ – 1 cup of distilled water (to your desired consistency)

Add ingredients to blender and blend until smooth. Refrigerate until chilled and enjoy. Makes about 4 servings.

THE TRUE SUSTENANCE

Our Savior and Lord is the Bread of Life. He sustains our life more than physical food ever will. He tells us in John 6:35, "I am the bread of life. Whoever comes to me will never go hungry, and whoever believes in me will never be thirsty" (NIV). During the fast, you will have times when you feel pangs of hunger or have cravings for foods that are not permitted. Consider each of these moments as a gift. Whenever you feel hungry, thirsty, or even if you have withdrawal symptoms, know that the Living Water and Bread of Life is beckoning you to come to Him. Pause intentionally and pray He fills your spirit before responding to your body physically. Go to His Word open and prepared to hear from Him. He is the God who loves to commune with us.

I used to have trouble praying, particularly in front of other people. I felt like I didn't know what to say and that I would stumble over my words or say the wrong thing. There was this unnecessary pressure that certainly did not come from God for me to pray these eloquent, sermon-like prayers. But He just wants our hearts, not pretense or flowery language. If you would like an example of a simple prayer that you can pray before eating either by yourself, with your family, or your children, here is one the Holy Spirit gave me:

God my Father, Loving One
I thank you for all that You've done
I'll live on every word You've said
Because You are my Daily Bread

You sent Jesus, Your only Son
So that my victory is won
And left with me Your Holy Ghost
So that I am never alone

And as I'm sitting down to eat
I thank you that You're here with me
Please bless our food, yes, every bite
And cover us in all Your might

In Jesus' name, I pray
Amen

God formed man from dust and breathed into him the breath of life (see Genesis 2:7). We are nothing without Him. There is no greater privilege and pleasure than to be close to the One who gave breath and is the infinite source of life and sustenance. Everything is from Him, through Him, and for Him that He may be glorified (see Romans 11:36), and we have the honor of walking with Him all of our days, if we will choose Him.

FOR MORE INFORMATION

For recipes and ideas for the Daniel Fast, visit jessicatucker.co or scan the QR code below. There you will find a community of people who are seeking God through fasting and want to share their ideas so that we can all do the same!

Part Two

DEVOTIONALS

Introduction

A devotional will accompany each day of this 21-day journey. Our goal is to seek the heart of God for His individual purpose of this specific fast and to place ourselves in the position to best hear from Him. Begin each day spending time with the Lord, reading the Word, and studying the devotional. There are questions presented at the end of each one to help stir our hearts and prompt us to both search ourselves and ask the Lord to search our hearts.

The Holy Spirit has a way of illuminating the Scriptures so we can read the same passage but get something different each time. Feel free to use these devotionals repeatedly as you complete additional Daniel fasts. I encourage you also to read the entire chapter and surrounding chapters that contain the passage referenced in each devotional. God reveals so much of Himself through our diligent study of His Word. There is a delight that springs up in us as we begin to understand and relate to the spiritual and practical concepts presented in the Scripture.

JOURNALING YOUR FAST

Before you start your fast, ask the Lord what He would like to speak to you, do through you, purge from you, or grow in you. Let Him know the desires of your heart. In what area(s) of your life are you longing to hear His voice? What do you desire to accomplish in the Kingdom? Where do you yearn to see breakthroughs in your family or experience healing in your heart, mind, or body?

Start a journal so you have these concepts in writing. Record your journey as you fast and watch the Hand of God move, touch, and transform you. The evidence will be all over the pages, and the journal will be precious to you for years to come. It can be difficult to remember all the things God does for us daily. Even aside from this fast, when He acts on your behalf, when He keeps His promises (as He always does), and when He fulfills that which He spoke, write it down. Write down when He says it, write down the process in between, and write down the fulfillment thereof.

I carry my journal with me everywhere I go. I sometimes flip to any page in it to remind myself of His goodness. That is not to say that every situation recorded on the pages is good, but He is always good. Lamentations says it this way in chapter 3, verses 21–26:

> ²¹ *This I recall to my mind, therefore have I hope.*
>
> ²² *It is of the Lord's mercies that we are not consumed, because his compassions fail not.*
>
> ²³ *They are new every morning: great is thy faithfulness.*
>
> ²⁴ *The Lord is my portion, saith my soul; therefore will I hope in him.*
>
> ²⁵ *The Lord is good unto them that wait for him, to the soul that seeketh him.*
>
> ²⁶ *It is good that a man should both hope and quietly wait for the salvation of the Lord (KJV).*

He holds it all together. I would have been utterly destroyed if He had not held back that which was after my life, my peace, and my joy. Keeping this journal will allow you to see the fulfillment of this passage in Lamentations. I love the phrase "we are not consumed." The Enemy does not want to just simply inconvenience us; he wants to destroy us by separating us from God.

The Enemy knows that if he can separate us from the Lord, he will rob us of our peace, strip away our testimony, and limit the drawing of other people to God. He has been trying to take the place of God since he was banished from heaven. Satan knows the power that our closeness with the Lord brings to us, and he wants to prevent that. The devil wants us to live in a way that is beneath what God has for us. If the Enemy cannot rob us of our eternity with God, he at least wants to rob us of the richness of life we can have on earth when we walk with the Lord.

Treasure your devotional time with the Lord. God could have chosen to make Himself inaccessible. He could have set all manner of parameter and boundary and requirement for reaching Him. But He didn't. He sent His Holy Spirit, and we can just talk with Him whenever we want. That is amazing to me. So, set the time apart. Give it priority. View it as sacred. And enjoy the response of the Lord as you make yourself available to Him.

JOURNAL DAY 0

1.   Lord, what do you want me to learn about You and Your Word during this fast?

2.   What truth(s) do You want to reveal to me about myself and my identity in You?

3.   What changes in my life do you want me to make to align myself better with Your will?

4.   How can I best honor You and serve your Kingdom in this season?

5.   Record any specific requests you have of Him for direction, healing, breakthrough, transformation, etc.

Be as transparent as possible in recording the answers to these questions. Sometimes we can be fearful of writing things down because we are concerned we did not hear God correctly or that our request will not align with what He wants. I encourage you to write it anyway. God is an immeasurably large God. He can use even that which we record in error to teach us something about Himself, His Word, or our identity in Him. He is not only God when we get it right. He is God all the time, and He can handle the human error He sent His Son to redeem.

THE DEVIL DIDN'T MAKE ME DO IT

Judges 6:1–6

¹ Then the children of Israel did evil in the sight of the Lord. So the Lord delivered them into the hand of Midian for seven years, ² and the hand of Midian prevailed against Israel. Because of the Midianites, the children of Israel made for themselves the dens, the caves, and the strongholds which are in the mountains. ³ So it was, whenever Israel had sown, Midianites would come up; also Amalekites and the people of the East would come up against them. ⁴ Then they would encamp against them and destroy the produce of the earth as far as Gaza, and leave no sustenance for Israel, neither sheep nor ox nor donkey. ⁵ For they would come up with their livestock and their tents, coming in as numerous as locusts; both they and their camels were without number; and they would enter the land to destroy it. ⁶ So Israel was greatly impoverished because of the Midianites, and the children of Israel cried out to the Lord (NKJV).

The Israelites suffered under Midianite oppression for seven years because of their disobedience and rebellion against the Lord. This oppression yielded poverty, lack, and despair in the hearts and lives of the Israelites. The Scriptures describe how their efforts toward improvement were consistently thwarted, their attempts at progress were blocked, and any increase they attained was decimated.

Prior to this season of Midianite oppression, the Lord brought the Israelites out of slavery in Egypt. He warned the Israelites not to submit to the gods of the land where they lived. The Israelites did not heed that warning or obey the command. They chose to place priority in something other than Him.

Some Old Testament depictions of idolatry are of a golden calf, belief in polytheistic deities, and the crafting of graven images. These examples of idolatry can seem much too blatant to be viewed as a warning against idolatry in our current context. But idolatry is simply placing anything or anyone before the One True God. This practice can be easy to fall into—particularly when the idol is more covert in nature. God expressly forbids this practice as His first of Ten Commandments to us is: "Thou shalt have no other gods before me" (Exodus 20:3 KJV).

A god we place before the True God can be success in the business world, financial security, our children, or the acceptance of others. It can be a significant other, status and prestige, or recognition. It is where we go first for comfort, for answers, or for affirmation.

The Israelites were in a very compromised position as they were being oppressed by the Midianites. Being in that situation could have felt like the Enemy was working hard against them to ensnare and entrap them. We often attribute negative situations to the devil or think that harmful thoughts always come from him.

This account illustrates a different perspective. The Bible says, "The Lord delivered them into the hand of Midian" (Judges 6:1 NKJV). In verse 10 of the same chapter, the Lord reminds the Israelites of His prior instruction to them not to worship the gods of the Amorites. He recounts that the Israelites did not listen to Him. The distinction that the Lord delivered the Israelites into Midianite hands brings up a principle we should internalize:

Not every negative scenario in which we find ourselves is the result of the Enemy at work.

Sometimes, God removes His hand from the situation. When God's hand is not present—when His hedge of protection does not surround an area of our lives—we are open to the natural consequences of our own decisions, the decisions of others, and the environment within which we are operating.

I remember like it was yesterday a season of my life when it felt like every small bit of increase I acquired—particularly financially—was almost immediately taken away. The dollar barely touched the inside of my palm before something snatched it. I felt like I was running at full speed; but the ground moved under me like the belt on a treadmill. I was exerting energy, but not changing my location—not moving forward.

I would think to myself: *The devil must really be after me.* Growing up in the church, I would hear "church-isms" like "The devil is busy." In the world, I would hear claims like "The devil made me do it." The devil is busy seeking to take ground away from the Kingdom of God. He wants to reduce, diminish, and destroy God's people. And he was after me. He has been all my life. But the devil was not the total blame for my season of financial lack.

> **NOT EVERY NEGATIVE SCENARIO IN WHICH WE FIND OURSELVES IS THE RESULT OF THE ENEMY AT WORK.**

In hindsight, I can see that part (maybe even the largest part) of the reason for my undesirable financial situation stemmed from an area of disobedience on my part.

God was not the Lord of my finances. And the devil didn't make me behave that way. I allowed fear to yield in me a reliance on my finite ability to produce and earn money over reliance on the sufficiency of God. I was focused so much on my lack that I could not see much aside from that. God tells us in His Word that He is Provider. He lets us know that in part because, when He asks something of us, we know He is so adequate to be all we need. We can trust Him in our obedience.

Part of making God Lord of my finances is obedience in returning the tithe to the storehouse. The first fruits (the first 10 percent) of all our increase belong to the Lord. And in His goodness, He attaches a promise in response to our obedience, written in Malachi 3:10–12:

¹⁰ Bring all the tithes into the storehouse,

That there may be food in My house,

And try Me now in this,"

Says the Lord of hosts,

"If I will not open for you the windows of heaven

And pour out for you such blessing

That there will not be room enough to receive it.

¹¹ "And I will rebuke the devourer for your sakes,

So that he will not destroy the fruit of your ground,

Nor shall the vine fail to bear fruit for you in the field,"

Says the Lord of hosts;

¹² "And all nations will call you blessed,

For you will be a delightful land,"

Says the Lord of hosts (NKJV).

I was not totally conscious of this at the time, but I felt like my resources were so restricted that I had nothing to spare. I idolized the pursuit of financial security over the pursuit of God. I was trying to be my own provider. I did not return the tithe. Natural consequences do not hold themselves back simply because we are unaware of them. They are natural. They occur automatically unless, of course, the Hand of God intervenes and says, *not so.*

My season of lack was not necessarily punitive, but it reflected what can happen when God's hand is not present. It is an illustration of what self-reliance produces versus what following God's plans produces.

The worst of my season of lack spanned five years. The next two years were a very slow and incremental walk in a better direction. The total was seven years. Similarly to the Israelites under Midianite oppression, I toiled to no avail. The devourer continually ate up whatever I grew.

The last phrase of Judges 6:6 is critical: "and the children of Israel cried out to the Lord." The people pleaded with the Lord to be released from this oppression, as it had infiltrated every part of their life and diminished them.

That crying out is an invitation that says, "Lord, You are welcome in this area of my life. I desire to walk in Your ways and live under Your Hand."

There was a process to their deliverance, but God did respond to their plea. He communicated to them the error they had made and then began working through a man named Gideon to facilitate their exodus from bondage. Their obedience began with Gideon building an altar to the Lord and destroying the altar of the false god, Baal.

Likewise, there was a process to my deliverance. That process helped to develop in me the character I would need to be able to live in abundance and give God the glory He is always due. It started with a crying out, an invitation to the Lord to reign over my whole life, including my finances. My obedience in returning the tithe and stewarding the Kingdom way followed, and the Lord kept His promise to rebuke the devourer for my sake.

We can conclude from this text that the Israelites' state of oppression with Midian was the result of their own actions—not the Enemy. It was a response to their disobedience of the first commandment. While the Enemy does seek to devour us, he is not always the author of our painful situations. When we live outside of the will of God in disobedience, we open ourselves up to the natural consequences of those actions.

God's mercy keeps us from receiving all the consequences we deserve. He gave His Son, so we do not have to pay the price for our sins. He paid it all. That's His mercy. But, when we remove ourselves from under His protective hand by being disobedient, we are not guaranteed protection from some of what we deserve.

We should seek to be obedient to God first because He loves us, and we love Him. This obedience should come with some ease when we consider His immeasurable love for us. 1 John 5:3 says, "For this is the love of God, that we keep his commandments: and his commandments are not grievous" (KJV). Other translations replace the word "grievous" with "burdensome."

Whenever we encounter an area of difficulty in obedience, we can be encouraged by setting our minds on the thoughts of all God has been to us and what He has done for and through us. Often, when I think through just a few of those concepts, I am overwhelmed and brought to tears. There is nothing He can ask of me that is too much.

He is so good. I can never repay Him for His goodness.

We can use these thoughts to guide us into joyful obedience because we know that His way is always the best way.

JOURNAL DAY 1

1.   What opportunities are there in my life to shift into a heart posture of obedience so I may give God lordship in that area?

2.   What areas of disobedience can I repent of and give over to God so I may live under His hand in that area?

3.   On this, the first day of the Daniel fast, how has God provided for me, changed my heart, revealed His heart to me, or revealed my heart to myself?

BUT WHO DOES HE SAY I AM?

¹¹ The angel of the Lord came and sat down under the oak in Ophrah that belonged to Joash the Abiezrite, where his son Gideon was threshing wheat in a winepress to keep it from the Midianites. ¹² When the angel of the Lord appeared to Gideon, he said, "The Lord is with you, mighty warrior."

¹³ "Pardon me, my lord," Gideon replied, "but if the Lord is with us, why has all this happened to us? Where are all his wonders that our ancestors told us about when they said, 'Did not the Lord bring us up out of Egypt?' But now the Lord has abandoned us and given us into the hand of Midian."

¹⁴ The Lord turned to him and said, "Go in the strength you have and save Israel out of Midian's hand. Am I not sending you?"

¹⁵ "Pardon me, my lord," Gideon replied, "but how can I save Israel? My clan is the weakest in Manasseh, and I am the least in my family."

¹⁶ The Lord answered, "I will be with you, and you will strike down all the Midianites, leaving none alive" (NIV).

After God revealed to the Israelites, through a prophet, the reason they were oppressed by the Midianites, He called an unlikely man by an unexpected name to deliver them out of Midianite bondage. The Angel of the Lord approached a man named Gideon, not on a battlefield or at a training ground, but hiding in a winepress, and called him a "mighty warrior" or "mighty man of valor."

Gideon's location at the time is significant. We know that while the Israelites were under Midianite oppression, it was common for the Midianites to steal and destroy the Israelites' crops. The crops were both a source of food and a vital part of the economic structure. A winepress is a place where grapes are pressed to make wine. That space was not used to harvest or "thresh" wheat. So, Gideon was hiding as he prepared the wheat. The Angel of the Lord called Gideon a name that was not consistent with his location, current behavior, or feelings.

This is a beautiful concept woven throughout Scripture that our loving Father exhibits. He finds and speaks to His people in places of fear, hiding, sickness, vulnerability, or sin and calls them a name that reflects how He sees them. For Gideon, it was calling him "mighty" as he hid in fear from his oppressor. For the woman who touched the hem of Jesus' garment to be healed of the issue of blood, it was calling her "Daughter" after she had spent 12 years existing on the fringes of society (see Luke 8:48). For Abraham, it was calling him the father of many nations when he and his wife were in their old age and could not naturally bear any children (see Genesis 17:5).

When the Angel of the Lord called Gideon, he responded by stating that he is the least in the family that is of the weakest clan in Israel. Gideon's perspective of himself, while based on facts about his family's lineage, was not reflective of the way God viewed him. God is aware of all facts, but is not limited by any fact. The key to fulfilling a purpose that surpasses our human limits rests in this: *We should seek to see ourselves how God sees us.*

Finding our identity in Him instead of culture, our families, our educational levels, or positions at work means that He will use us to do that which is greater than us. We should listen to what God calls us—even if we do not see the evidence of it in the present moment. God called Gideon mighty before he had even gone to battle. He was able to call him that because He knew that He, the All-Sufficient One, would be with Gideon through the battle.

> # WE SHOULD SEEK TO SEE OURSELVES HOW GOD SEES US.

Since God knows our hearts, He already knew that Gideon felt inadequate. God did not wait until Gideon had data to support His statement to speak it to Gideon. God does not lead us to simply gather facts in support of His Word; He wants us to have faith that His Word is true and final. God's timing was perfect so that when Gideon recalled this encounter, He could credit only God for his might. Gideon would remember that space of weakness and know that the victory had to have been the Lord's.

God loves to use us in our space of weakness. It brings Him glory. The Scriptures tell us in 2 Corinthians 12:9 that His strength is made perfect in our weakness. So we can find joy and peace in the areas of our inadequacy if we will submit those areas to Him. He can make miracles out of them.

Years ago, I worked as a social worker in a facility where recently incarcerated individuals lived. The men who lived there had all been incarcerated for the same category of crime. Part of my role was to approve or disapprove the movement of individuals outside of the facility in which they were housed. I was the youngest person on staff and the least experienced.

I hid my age well, but I was continuously aware that as an inexperienced temp worker, there was little room for error. There was an individual housed within the facility who requested to leave at a specific time to go to a particular place. His requests were definitive and eager. Too eager.

When the request came to me for signature, I felt uneasy—to say the least. I could not shake the feeling that by approving the request, I would endanger someone else. I held the clipboard on which the request was placed, and my hand trembled as I moved pen to paper. I couldn't sign it.

I prepared myself for the staff meeting where I knew they would pressure me to sign. The leadership of the organization was notorious for wanting to keep their hands clean of any responsibility, while pressuring those at the working level to make impossible decisions or lose their job. They were crafty enough to make sure that the pressure applied was covert and untraceable—therefore making it unreportable.

A supervisor told me they were tired of receiving complaints from the person whose request I denied. This is the same supervisor who frequently reminded me that I was young and inexperienced and could not possibly understand the nuances and dynamics of the field in which I worked. That supervisor slid the request across the table in the middle of the meeting in front of all the staff and demanded, "Sign it."

I refused.

I explained that I felt I would be putting others in danger by approving it. I may have been young and inexperienced, but I knew that this person with this request would re-offend. He had his sights set on a new victim. I let the supervisor know that if they wanted it approved, they would have to sign it themselves. The air left the room. I could see the clenched jaw and the vein in their foreheads. I knew at that moment I had lost my job.

We may see ourselves a certain way because of the feedback we have received over the years. We may have even been called names, underestimated, minimized, or labeled certain things by others. Maybe some of those labels and names feel true.

But who does He say I am?

God knew that I was young and inexperienced when He sent me to perform that role. He also knew He could trust me to take a stand, even though I knew it would mean losing my job.

I would love to tell you that because I did not sign, the individual was denied his request, did not re-offend, and I kept my job. None of that was the case. The supervisor approved the request, and the person re-offended—just as I feared. I was comforted by the fact that a Good Samaritan stepped in and helped to protect the would-be victim of the crime that was about to be committed against them. I believe the Lord sent that person to protect them.

They let me go from my job shortly after. I had never been fired from anything in my life. When I was given the news that I was being fired, I felt no regret. I was glad I took a stand. I prayed God would use that stand to inspire those who witnessed it so they would also stand up when their time came to do so.

It probably looked to some like I did not win the victory. But I did. I was walking in who God says I am. And since He owns the cattle on a thousand hills (see Psalm 50:10), He has an endless supply with which to replace that which was lost.

I was hired at another, much better job in less than a month. The role was work that I enjoyed, the compensation was better, and I felt like I was making a difference. I was able to move into that role with dignity, knowing I obeyed the voice of the Lord. In my new position, no one brought up how young or inexperienced I was. In fact, part of why they hired me was because I recounted the stand I took on that previous position during my interview. One interviewer would later be in my leadership chain. My courage and integrity moved her, and she thanked me for thinking of others outside of myself.

I don't think that I mentioned the Lord directly in that interview, but I found out later that she knew I loved the Lord simply by the way I told the story. There are testimonies the world needs to hear from us. Our decisions affect much more than just us.

The Angel of the Lord called Gideon to save Israel from the Midianites. In His call, the Lord called Gideon mighty and favored. As we read about Gideon in that passage, we pick up on statements made by him that seem hesitant or even fearful. We may find ourselves able to relate to statements he made and questions he had for God. Gideon initially could not fathom how he, who is described by words like "weakest" and "least," could possibly save Israel. God did not scold Gideon for asking for a sign of confirmation that He was with Him. God honored that request. After the Lord sent the signs, Gideon and many men gathered in preparation for battle with the Midianites.

Gideon built an altar to the Lord based upon the word of the Lord—before any battle against the Midianites was won. The Lord spoke peace over Gideon, and Gideon responded by building an altar to the Lord and calling it "The-Lord-*Is*-Peace."

God's word is enough.

Once He says it, we can depend on it right then. We can call it finished, completed, and true because He is faithful. And if He begins it, He will complete it. He tells us so in His Word: "Being confident of this very thing, that He who has begun a good work in you will complete it until the day of Jesus Christ" (Philippians 1:6 NKJV).

1.   What has God called me to that I do not feel sufficient to accomplish?

2.   What part of God's character can I stand on to replace feelings of inadequacy?

3.   On Day 2 of the fast, what areas of weakness are being revealed to me, and how can I allow God to get glory in those spaces?

IT'S SMALL, BUT IT'S ENOUGH

[1] Then Jerubbaal (that is, Gideon) and all the people who were with him rose early and encamped beside the well of Harod, so that the camp of the Midianites was on the north side of them by the hill of Moreh in the valley.

[2] And the Lord said to Gideon, "The people who are with you are too many for Me to give the Midianites into their hands, lest Israel claim glory for itself against Me, saying, 'My own hand has saved me.' [3] Now therefore, proclaim in the hearing of the people, saying, 'Whoever is fearful and afraid, let him turn and depart at once from Mount Gilead.'" And twenty-two thousand people returned, and ten thousand remained.

[4] But the Lord said to Gideon, "The people are still too many; bring them down to the water, and I will test them for you there. Then it will be, that of whom I say to you, 'This one shall go with you,' the same shall go with you; and of whomever I say to you, 'This one shall not go with you,' the same shall not go." [5] So he brought the people down to the water. And the Lord said to Gideon, "Everyone who laps from the water with his tongue, as a dog laps, you shall set apart by himself; likewise everyone who gets down on his knees to drink." [6] And the number of those who lapped, putting their hand to their mouth, was three hundred men; but all the rest of the people got down on their knees to drink water. [7] Then the Lord said to Gideon, "By the three hundred men who lapped I will save you, and deliver the Midianites into your hand. Let all the other people go, every man to his place." [8] So the people took provisions and their trumpets in their hands. And he sent away all the rest of Israel, every man to his tent, and retained those three hundred men. Now the camp of Midian was below him in the valley (NKJV).

The seven-year bondage of the Israelites under the Midianites was devastating to the Israelites. The Scriptures describe the depths of despair and desperation they experienced during their enslavement. It would seem that such a powerful and oppressive enemy would need to be met with an even larger, more powerful army to be overthrown.

The Scriptures describe about 32,000 people who were initially assembled to prepare for battle against the Midianites. When the Lord spoke to Gideon about the battle to come, He did not begin by discussing how to train soldiers for war or how to organize such a large group in a way that optimized their chances for victory. He did not discuss how to raise the people up to be great enough in their own strength. Instead, he instructed Gideon to tell those who were afraid to leave the place where they were assembled. That instruction left them with 10,000 people.

The 10,000 that remained was significantly less than the initial 32,000, but one could still imagine winning a battle with a group of that size. God saw that as still too much. Often, if we can rationalize how we have accomplished a thing, we can think that we possess the power within ourselves and we do not need God's grace. To prevent breeding self-sufficiency in their hearts, the Lord called for another test, which resulted in another reduction. This time, all that remained were 300 men.

I've never organized an army for war. I don't know the first thing about military warfare and what it takes to defeat an enemy of the magnitude of the Midianites. I wouldn't know where to begin drawing up plans or how to determine the criteria for whom to choose to fight in the army. But one thing I know is this: 300 men are not enough.

As I study the Scriptures, I have noticed a pattern. In 2 Kings 4, there is an account of a widow who lost her husband and feared she would lose her sons to slavery to pay the debt her family owed. They no longer had the head and provider of their house. She went to the prophet Elisha and described her predicament.

He responded by asking her what she had in her house. She said, "Your maidservant has nothing in the house but a jar of oil" (2 Kings 4:2 NKJV). Her response was a sort of discount—a minimization of what she possessed. She spoke the word "nothing" before describing the jar of oil.

Even though she described the jar of oil as if it was insignificant, the prophet responded to her with instructions. He told her to gather other jars from her neighbors, go in the house and shut the door, and pour the oil into the jars. She did so and filled all the jars that were brought into her house with the oil. The prophet then said, "Sell the oil and pay your debt; and you *and* your sons live on the rest: (2 Kings 4:7 NKJV).

God took her little and made it much.

One more example of this pattern in Scripture is found in each of the Gospels. One version, told in Matthew 14, describes a scene where Jesus was before a large crowd until evening. There were 5,000 men plus women and children, and they were hungry. The disciples reported this to Jesus, who told them to get the people something to eat. All the disciples could find was a lunch of five loaves of bread and two fish. Jesus took it, blessed it, broke it, and gave the food to the disciples. The disciples gave it to the people. Jesus performed a miracle that day, in that the people all ate until they were full, and there were 12 baskets of leftovers.

Three hundred men against an entire nation is not enough to win a battle and break out of oppression. One small jar of oil is not enough to sustain financially and economically a family of three. One lunch of five loaves of bread and two fish is not enough to feed a multitude of 5,000 men plus women and children.

But each of these accounts ends in a victory that delineates a beautiful picture: *Even if it's small, it's enough if God is with us.*

When God called me to write this book, He gave me a release date before He gave me any content of the book. I did not have a publisher. I had no knowledge of how to write a book, and I didn't have enough time (in my mind) to complete the book by the release date He ordained.

When He showed me who the publisher would be, she gave me a deadline for completion of the book. It was even less time than the "already-not-enough" I had initially contemplated. I felt nervous, but I could imagine how that timeline was in the realm of possible. I could use my skill set to accomplish it.

Then she cut the timeline back again. This time, to an impossibly short duration. When I saw the email, I put away the items I was using at the gym mid-workout and went to sit in my car and despair. No one writes a book that fast. I thought surely the Lord would tell me I did not have to complete the book in such a short period of time.

EVEN IF IT'S SMALL, IT'S ENOUGH IF GOD IS WITH US.

He did not. He said to do it. He said He would give me the words and make the time enough. He showed me Gideon and the 300 men. He gave me a word that would be unbelievable if anyone other than Him said it.

If God would have allowed either of the first two timelines to remain in place, the testimony I would have to tell would not be that of a miracle. It would appear that a person simply utilized efficiently the skills God gave. That is not the story the Lord was writing.

God needed it to be clear that this work was His doing—not mine. He loves us too much to let us build our faith on the foundation of our own abilities, resources, and strengths. That is a foundation that will surely shift and crumble. Psalm 18:2 says, "The Lord is my rock, my fortress and my deliverer; my God is my rock, in whom I take refuge, my shield and the horn of my salvation, my stronghold" (NIV). His is a foundation that cannot be moved.

God loves to use our too little, too small, and not enough. He loves to use our limitations and weaknesses. They are the best platforms to display His boundless power and infiniteness. He enjoys allowing for impossible situations to show up so He can place His Hand on them and transform them.

He is the God of multiplication. He will not only make it enough, but He can make it overflow. God kept His promise to Gideon to deliver the Midianites into his hand. They not only won the battle but were also delivered out of oppression. God sustained the widow and her family for the rest of their days with the multiplication of one small jar of oil. He fed the entire multitude and had baskets filled with leftovers. He empowered me to write this book and meet the impossible deadline.

It is much more comfortable to approach a difficult task with enough effort in the natural. We want to have enough people, enough expertise, enough money, enough foresight to walk into difficult situations with confidence. We sometimes forget that the best advantage we could have has nothing to do with the resources we bring to the battle. Rather, it is *Who* speaks over the situation in the first place. All the best resources in the world are no match to The Almighty God. No resource can be superior to The Source. We are better to face situations empty-handed with God than totally prepared in the natural, without God.

JOURNAL DAY 3

1. In what circumstances can I shift to trusting God over my own resources and/or abilities?

2. Identify areas of strength that could make you susceptible to falling into self-sufficiency or pride.

3. Recall the times that God has made more than enough out of too little.

Often, day three is when people want to quit the Daniel fast. That was the make-or-break day during my first fast. I want to encourage you not to quit. God has all the strength, endurance, and peace that you need. Seek Him, and He will give those to you.

Devotional Day 4:

FAVOR VERSUS FAIRNESS

¹ Now Jacob dwelt in the land where his father was a stranger, in the land of Canaan. ² This is the history of Jacob.

Joseph, being seventeen years old, was feeding the flock with his brothers. And the lad was with the sons of Bilhah and the sons of Zilpah, his father's wives; and Joseph brought a bad report of them to his father.

³ Now Israel loved Joseph more than all his children, because he was the son of his old age. Also, he made him a tunic of many colors. ⁴ But when his brothers saw that their father loved him more than all his brothers, they hated him and could not speak peaceably to him.

⁵ Now Joseph had a dream, and he told it to his brothers; and they hated him even more (NKJV).

Joseph's father Jacob had 13 children—12 sons and one daughter. Of those 13, Joseph was his favorite because he was born when Jacob was old. As a token and representation of his favor, he made Joseph a tunic, or coat, of many colors. Joseph's brothers became aware their father favored Joseph over all of them, and they hated Joseph for it. They hated Joseph even more when they heard the dreams he was having that they interpreted to mean Joseph would rule over them. Their jealousy swelled to where they created a plan to kill him.

It is interesting how specific the Scriptures are describing the hatred Joseph's brothers had toward him. Joseph received the favor of his father because of something about him that he could not control. Joseph had nothing to do with the timing of his own birth. His father favored him over all his other children. Instead of his brothers turning their frustration toward the one who made the decision to elevate one child over the rest, they harbored resentment toward the object of their father's favor, Joseph.

Their hatred increased when Joseph began to utilize a God-given gift—the interpretation of dreams. Joseph had the favor of both his earthly and heavenly Father. His brothers had to witness the evidence of both: the coat of many colors from Jacob and the gift of dream interpretation from God. His brothers could have been happy for their brother, simply because he was family and they loved him. They made a different choice.

Joseph's familial situation reveals the other side of one of the blessings of God: *Favor can bring unwanted attention from others in the form of jealousy.*

Joseph was just a boy—17 years old—and his brothers thought to take his very life because they were jealous. This is unsettling for many reasons, and it also feels very unfair. Joseph did not *cause* his father to favor him over his brothers. He did not *cause* God to bless him with a gift. Yet, he had become a target of his siblings.

The favor of God is a gift we cannot earn. It is unmerited. It is given to us because we are God's children. So, sometimes, onlookers will see the evidence of this favor on our lives and become resentful or envious. Notice I said onlookers—not unbelievers. Unfortunately, some of this resentment can come from fellow believers.

> **FAVOR CAN BRING UNWANTED ATTENTION FROM OTHERS IN THE FORM OF JEALOUSY.**

When we choose a consecrated, God-centered life, we can unintentionally hold a mirror to those around us—especially fellow believers who are called to do the same. Some believers who struggle with allowing God lordship in their lives may resent those who live in that space. It is especially painful when the resentment comes from a family member, pastor, church member, close friend, or any person we would reasonably expect to have our best interests at heart.

Many years ago, when I was a teenager, I received some feedback that I will never forget. Most of the conversation is now a blur of sound bites and memory echoes, but one statement remains vividly in my mind. I was told, "Some people don't like you because you are the mirror they don't want to look in."

I remember feeling stunned, uneasy, and confused. I stayed to myself. I was very private, and I made so many mistakes. What could possibly bother people that much about me? I was just a kid.

His favor was on my life, even back then. Over the years, I have experienced what I now call the "mirror effect" over and over again. At first, I could not wrap my mind around it because all that would come to my mind is how flawed I am, how much I get wrong, and how long my list of disappointments is. What I have now learned is that it is the submission to the Holy Spirit that people resent. It is the conviction they feel that they dislike. But I am just a vessel He chose to use.

One of the most impactful experiences I had with this was at a church. Some time ago, I served on the worship team of a church. God called me to that place. I had my reservations about being a part of that particular church body, but I was determined to obey the Lord. As the years went by, the Holy Spirit began to show me a dangerous trend. The Enemy was infiltrating the worship team and the church leadership with the demonic spirit of pride. It was frightening to observe.

I watched as those who initially seemed to want to serve the Lord morphed into self-serving, attention-seeking, power-hungry people. Please don't read what I am not writing. This is not a judgment of the people in that church. It is an observation of fruit. The Bible says in Matthew 7:15–20 that we know a tree by its fruit. Likewise, there are things we know about people by the fruit they bear.

The Holy Spirit revealed to me that part of why He placed me there was to speak up about the pride spirit He had revealed to me. I knew what that would mean for my future within that church body. I had experienced this many times before.

I followed the procedure for raising a spiritual concern within the church. At first, there was a glimmer of hope that the church leadership and worship team would be receptive to the feedback. I began teaching a Bible study on the heart of worship, seeking God each time on how to communicate how He wants us to revere Him, worship Him, and put Him first.

We must always remember that the Enemy does not let his grasp of people go easily—especially if he has made great headway in the House of God. Once there was a shift in the heart of the pastor at the hand of the Enemy, everyone else (with the exception of one other person) followed suit.

I still cannot adequately describe how painful it was to hear the pastor I once respected as a spiritual leader cast me down, malign my character, and eventually invite me to leave the worship team and the church. Other people there were so afraid of him that they either joined in and sided with him or sat in silence, allowing it to happen.

These are people who for years I ministered with, prayed for, visited when they were sick, laid hands on when they were in distress. They could not even give a clear answer as to what I did wrong to deserve this treatment. I had done nothing wrong. They simply allowed the Enemy to lead them down the wrong path. I was the mirror they didn't want to look in, and I wanted God to get the glory, not me.

I won't recount all that was said and done to me, but I assure you, it was horrific. The Enemy would whisper to me reminders of what was happening. All day, he talked to me. I was told that nothing I did there mattered. He said that the ugly things the pastor said about me were true, and he asked me, "What kind of person gets put out of a *church*?" He reminded me that only one person was with me and said that we were no match against such a large church. He wanted me to take my life, or at least never return to any church or ministry ever again.

They were supposed to be my family, and they betrayed me.

I even had proof of what was said. I remember one day, I was praying. I had all my proof compiled and said, "Ok God, whom do I need to send this to?"

"No one," He said. "You have to let Me take care of it."

No one! I told God how this was an open and shut case! I could just solve it! They would be exposed, and His people freed from that deception of the Enemy. And I would be vindicated! It would be one thing if I did not have ironclad proof, but I did. This would have been too easy!

He reminded me of what He says in His Word in Romans 12:19: "Dearly beloved, avenge not yourselves, but rather give place unto wrath: for it is written, Vengeance is mine; I will repay, saith the Lord" (KJV).

The NIV translation says it this way: "Leave room for God's wrath."

If we take vengeance upon ourselves, we take that room away from God. Peace washed over me as I realized: God will take care of it. And He will do it in the most optimal and right way.

It takes a work of the Lord to give us the grace to not retaliate in kind when we are mistreated because of the favor of God. Fortunately for us, He tells us in His Word that His grace is sufficient for us (see 2 Corinthians 12:9). We must lean on Him in these times and allow Him to guide our hands and our words, so we do not repay unkindness with more unkindness.

Removal from that church ended up being an immeasurable blessing, just as Joseph was eventually richly blessed after being sold into slavery by his brothers. We must choose to trust God's plan and His infinite ability. He truly does work all things "together for good to them that love God, to them who are the called according to his purpose" (Romans 8:28 KJV).

Someone else's refusal to resist the devil is not a reflection of me. That belongs completely to them. Even if the person is in the church and their refusal to resist ends up in harm to me, that is still not my burden to bear. We are the church. So, if a particular church building and its members or leadership fail, that is okay. I can be the church anyway.

JOURNAL DAY 4

1. Recall times when God's handling of a situation far superseded your own solution—even when you did not see it that way at first.

2. Do I trust God to protect me even when the resentment I experience from others is from fellow believers, the church body, and/or family members?

3. Am I willing to stand alone to follow the commandment of God?

Devotional Day 5:

HE'S STILL GOOD

²³ So it came to pass, when Joseph had come to his brothers, that they stripped Joseph of his tunic, the tunic of many colors that was on him. ²⁴ Then they took him and cast him into a pit. And the pit was empty; there was no water in it.

²⁵ And they sat down to eat a meal. Then they lifted their eyes and looked, and there was a company of Ishmaelites, coming from Gilead with their camels, bearing spices, balm, and myrrh, on their way to carry them down to Egypt.

²⁶ So Judah said to his brothers, "What profit is there if we kill our brother and conceal his blood? ²⁷ Come and let us sell him to the Ishmaelites, and let not our hand be upon him, for he is our brother and our flesh." And his brothers listened. ²⁸ Then Midianite traders passed by; so the brothers pulled Joseph up and lifted him out of the pit, and sold him to the Ishmaelites for twenty shekels of silver. And they took Joseph to Egypt.

²⁹ Then Reuben returned to the pit, and indeed Joseph was not in the pit; and he tore his clothes. ³⁰ And he returned to his brothers and said, "The lad is no more; and I, where shall I go?"

³¹ So they took Joseph's tunic, killed a kid of the goats, and dipped the tunic in the blood. ³² Then they sent the tunic of many colors, and they brought it to their father and said, "We have found this. Do you know whether it is your son's tunic or not?"

³³ And he recognized it and said, "It is my son's tunic. A wild beast has devoured him. Without doubt Joseph is torn to pieces." ³⁴ Then Jacob tore his clothes, put sackcloth on his waist, and mourned for his son many days. ³⁵ And all his sons and all his daughters arose to comfort him; but he refused to be comforted, and he said, "For I shall go down into the grave to my son in mourning." Thus his father wept for him.

³⁶ Now the Midianites had sold him in Egypt to Potiphar, an officer of Pharaoh and captain of the guard (NKJV).

Joseph's brothers' initial plan was to kill him because they were so envious of him. However, one of Joseph's brothers, Reuben, convinced them not to kill Joseph and instead throw him into a pit. Following that, the brothers saw an opportunity and sold Joseph to the Ishmaelites. They took from Joseph the token of his father's favor—his coat of many colors. They dipped it in blood to deceive their father into believing animals had killed his son. Jacob was so overcome with grief at the loss of his precious son that he was inconsolable.

After such evil, cruelty, and trauma at the hands of his own brothers, one may think that Joseph would not have to encounter that manner of devastation ever again. We might think—*that's enough. He paid his dues.* That was not the case. Joseph again found favor, but this time with Potiphar, to whom they sold him in Egypt. Potiphar set him over his house and everything he had. But Potiphar's wife saw Joseph, desired him, and said to him, "lie with me" (Genesis 39:7 NKJV).

Joseph refused her advances, but she persisted. Eventually, she grabbed him by the garment he was wearing and instructed him again to lie with her. He refused and ran away, leaving that garment behind. Potiphar's wife used the garment to deceive Potiphar into thinking that Joseph was the one making the advances. As a result, they sent him to prison.

With the mistreatment at the hands of his brothers not far in the rearview, the deception of Potiphar's wife adds insult to injury. He was sent to prison because she was attracted to and behaved inappropriately toward him. He did nothing to bring that upon himself. The coupling of these two parts of Joseph's life shows us this: *Experiencing a deeply traumatic, unfair situation does not automatically release us from experiencing another—maybe even one similar to the last.*

Joseph was sold into slavery at the hands of his brothers and then was thrown into prison for doing the right thing by refusing the advances of his leader's wife. Satan loves to use our fatigue in difficult and repetitive situations to set up roots of bitterness in our lives. If he can establish that root, it can grow into a lack of trust in God and a distorted perception of His goodness. It can also damage our ability to enter healthy relationships with others by convincing us that no one can be trusted.

The situation I mentioned in yesterday's devotional was not the first time I had experienced church hurt. I spent several years in succession not attending church, for fear that I would be harmed again. During those years, I found a church I thought I might like. I experienced more hurt there, which solidified my escape from the church.

So, as you can imagine, when I returned to church after a decade of being away, I was apprehensive. The trauma I experienced after years of faithful service within that church threatened to undo me. To make matters worse, that church and its pastor were not the only betrayal, rejection, and trauma I was experiencing at that time. A friend I thought I knew began to show a dark, manipulative side that took my breath away in the worst way. Also, a family member who ought to love me was constructing a plan for my downfall on purpose.

I remember a weight that sat heavily on my neck and shoulders. These three men I should have been able to trust and rely on pulled the ground out from under my feet. The Enemy began using the family member to attack me when I was a very little girl.

His goal was to annihilate my self-esteem, hinder my faith, thwart my purpose, and stall my walk with God. The Enemy placed the seed of envy in this family member much like the one that was planted in Joseph's brothers.

> **EXPERIENCING A DEEPLY TRAUMATIC, UNFAIR SITUATION DOES NOT AUTOMATICALLY RELEASE US FROM EXPERIENCING ANOTHER.**

Once the Enemy has instilled that jealousy in a person, they can do things to a person that are unimaginable. They are both fueled by and blinded to their jealousy—which is a dangerous combination. I had to learn that even though this person was a key person in my familial landscape, he did not have the final say on who I am. God does. And since he was being influenced by the Enemy, who is a liar, I can rest in the truth of God and resist the lies the Enemy tells through him.

Since the devil failed in destroying me in my formative years using that family member, he not only doubled down in his efforts with that family member but also did so with my former pastor and a close friend. He had to multiply his efforts.

Sometimes, I felt this was unfair. Sometimes, I wondered what I could have done to deserve those experiences. Have you had similar experiences? Maybe you were betrayed by a parent, sibling, or best friend. Maybe your pastor or other leader failed you in a way that threatened to shift your perspective on life and even God. It's even worse when there is one trauma after another.

Negative experiences with people can shake our faith to its core. But one perspective on which I focused was this: *God must be preparing to use me in a powerful way, and the Enemy is terrified.* Why would he work that hard unless he was extremely threatened? We must remember that the devil has been around a long time. He sees patterns that alert him to those who most threaten his work.

Sometimes, when I am in a difficult season, I pray: *Thank You, Lord, for trusting me not just with blessing but with trouble. And thank You for sustaining me in this season.*

I love how it is said in Lamentations 3:21–24:

21 This I recall to my mind,

Therefore I have hope.

22 Through the Lord's mercies we are not consumed,

Because His compassions fail not.

23 They are new every morning;

Great is Your faithfulness.

24 "The Lord is my portion," says my soul,

"Therefore I hope in Him!" (KJV).

I would have fallen apart at the seams if it were not for the Lord. Satan tried to isolate me so he could say anything he wanted to say to me. Joseph endured isolation and bondage too—in slavery and in imprisonment. The time between enslavement at age 17 and rising to power at age 30 probably felt like an eternity. It was likely exhausting and draining in many aspects.

When I am tired and under attack, Psalm 27:13 comes to mind: "I had fainted, unless I had believed to see the goodness of the Lord in the land of the living" (KJV). He is still good. The circumstance is not always good, but He is above the circumstance. I don't have to let the actions of others erode my foundation in Christ. He is the Solid Rock. I can put my whole weight on Him, and He is not moved.

The same way God was with us in the first trauma, He will stay with us through the next and the next. Joseph may have been rejected by family, leaders, and mentors, but God was with him in the pit and in the prison. And He remained with him when he ascended to power in Pharaoh's house.

He has remained with me through rejection by natural family, church family, and friendship. He never left me alone, but placed Himself in the forefront of my perspective so that I would not succumb to the pressure of the mistreatment. God is immutable—unchanging. He was good. He is good. and He will be good. Nothing catches Him by surprise. He tells us we will have trouble in this world, but we can be comforted in the fact that He has overcome the world (see John 16:33).

1.   Am I prioritizing praying for the endurance that God gives so I may outlast the trials of this world?

2.   Do I believe God is still good when the situation is not good?

3.   What troubles have I encountered during the fast that can point me still to the goodness of God?

Devotional Day 6:

HE CAN REPLACE THE COAT

³⁷ So the advice was good in the eyes of Pharaoh and in the eyes of all his servants. ³⁸ And Pharaoh said to his servants, "Can we find such a one as this, a man in whom is the Spirit of God?"

³⁹ Then Pharaoh said to Joseph, "Inasmuch as God has shown you all this, there is no one as discerning and wise as you. ⁴⁰ You shall be over my house, and all my people shall be ruled according to your word; only in regard to the throne will I be greater than you." ⁴¹ And Pharaoh said to Joseph, "See, I have set you over all the land of Egypt."

⁴² Then Pharaoh took his signet ring off his hand and put it on Joseph's hand; and he clothed him in garments of fine linen and put a gold chain around his neck. ⁴³ And he had him ride in the second chariot which he had; and they cried out before him, "Bow the knee!" So he set him over all the land of Egypt. ⁴⁴ Pharaoh also said to Joseph, "I am Pharaoh, and without your consent no man may lift his hand or foot in all the land of Egypt." ⁴⁵ And Pharaoh called Joseph's name Zaphnath-Paaneah. And he gave him as a wife Asenath, the daughter of Poti-Pherah priest of On. So Joseph went out over all the land of Egypt.

⁴⁶ Joseph was thirty years old when he stood before Pharaoh king of Egypt. And Joseph went out from the presence of Pharaoh, and went throughout all the land of Egypt (NKJV).

Genesis 41 describes a dream that greatly troubled Pharaoh. He asked magicians and wise men to help him interpret the meaning of his dreams, but no one could. The Pharaoh's chief butler recalled a time when Joseph interpreted dreams while in prison. Pharaoh called for Joseph, and he was brought forth to interpret the Pharaoh's dreams.

Joseph informed Pharaoh that through his dreams, God was showing Pharaoh what He was about to do. There would be seven years of plenty in the land, followed by seven years of famine. He advised Pharaoh to appoint a man of wisdom to help him prepare for the fulfillment of this word from the Lord.

This advice brought Joseph favor in the eyes of Pharaoh. Pharaoh acknowledged God had shown Joseph the meaning of his dreams. Pharaoh placed Joseph in authority over his house and the land of Egypt. Pharaoh gave him a ring, fine linens to wear, and a gold chain for his neck. Joseph was appointed to direct the people in the land in preparation for and walking through a multi-year famine.

People from other lands came to Egypt to buy food during the famine. Among those who would come were Joseph's brothers. But God used Joseph to keep his brothers from starving. He did so—even though his brothers did not offer him that same kindness years earlier.

There was a process between being sold into slavery at age 17 and being promoted into authority of all the land at age 30. If the latter had occurred at the beginning of Joseph's journey, he might not have been properly developed to handle it. What that tells us is this: *If we will trust God through the highs and the lows of our processes, He will strengthen our character and use us for His glory.*

At the age of 16, I left home to go face the world on my own. The circumstances surrounding my early departure were not all positive, but God would do many miracles using that season. The years that followed were shrouded in lack, despair, bondage, and rejection. It felt like a perpetual boxing match. I wasn't getting knocked out, but I sure was tired.

After so many years of development by fire, I wondered when I would get to experience something positive. I wanted to know when I would be accepted and not rejected for the gifting God had so generously bestowed upon me. I pondered if I would ever be seen.

I would experience that at 30 years old.

That year, there was a particular service I needed to hire a firm to accomplish for me. I began researching different firms and investigated a list of five of them. I interviewed each firm, not totally aware of how I would choose the right one. In my heart, I knew God would show me the right one.

Throughout my interviews of firms, I met the presumptuous, the overly eager, and the dismissive. But there was one firm that stood out to me. I spoke with someone in the office before setting a time to meet with the firm's owner. I remember feeling uplifted following that conversation—not overwhelmed and discouraged like I had felt after some of the others.

> **IF WE WILL TRUST GOD THROUGH THE HIGHS AND THE LOWS OF OUR PROCESSES, HE WILL STRENGTHEN OUR CHARACTER AND USE US FOR HIS GLORY.**

I met with the owner and was impressed with his presentation, work ethic, and approach to business. I was even more moved by the fact that he ran a faith-based business. It was refreshing that he seemed to be genuinely interested in my life, skill set, and character. He wanted to provide the service that I needed. I felt in my spirit that his was the firm I was going to hire.

During our meeting, he asked me if I had ever considered working in that field. It was a field in which I was highly interested, but I had never imagined I would be capable of performing that type of work. I gave him a non-answer. He then further asked if I would consider working in his firm. I sort of laughed because I didn't think he was serious. This was the very first time we had met. I told him I needed to pray about my decision on which firm I would hire, and I would get back to him.

A few months later, I was at home praying about what God wanted me to do next. I felt His nudging toward something; I just didn't know what it was. I prayed He would make it clear so I would only do what He was calling me to do—nothing else. As soon as I said "Amen," the owner of the firm I had met with earlier called me.

He said he was serious about the question he asked me when we had that first meeting. He wanted to know if I would come and work there. I felt the Holy Spirit speak confirmation in my spirit in that moment. All the previous fears and inadequacies washed away. I knew this was the answer to my prayer. I immediately told him, "Yes."

God accelerated the process for me to learn about the industry and pass the test to be appropriately licensed. Our firm moved our main office to another location as I started working in my new position. I remember sitting in a beautiful, newly furnished corner office sobbing out of pure gratefulness for the favor and faithfulness of God.

 God did that for me after one meeting. He placed me on this person's heart and moved him to act because of it. In that moment, God redeemed and restored me from so much prior mistreatment and rejection. He showed me that He can place me in the right position at the right time because He is in control. "The king's heart is in the hand of the Lord, as the rivers of water: he turneth it whithersoever he will" (Proverbs 21:1 KJV).

I cannot take any credit. The owner of that firm is a discerning businessman. He makes wise and calculated decisions. He would not be frivolous in choosing someone for that position—especially since he needed to plan for the next generation of leadership of his firm. The time between 16 and 30 was not at all wasted. It was a training ground to prepare me to walk in the favor of God in a miraculous way later.

There are things we desire that we do not yet have the character to support. This same principle has many other applications. There may be a project we want to accomplish that we will not be able to accomplish until we acquire the right skill set. Maybe there is a sport in which we want to participate that we will not be able to engage in until our body is adequately conditioned for it. Maybe there is a relationship we want to have that we will not be able to steward correctly until we experience healing in a certain area.

When God allows trials in our lives, we should not immediately assume that a trial is punitive. In fact, the book of James says, "Consider it pure joy, my brothers and sisters, whenever you face trials of many kinds, because you know that the testing of your faith produces perseverance. Let perseverance finish its work so that you may be mature and complete, not lacking anything" (James 1:2–4 NIV).

I am grateful for the road that led me into that new season. Had I not experienced trials, I might have ruined the blessings He gave me. In that role, I sometimes had to help people who had previously mistreated me. Without that developmental time, I would not have had the strength and faith to do so gracefully and without malice or complaint. Let us endeavor to trust what God allows, and lean into Him to sustain us through it.

When Joseph was thrown into the pit, his brothers took the physical evidence of his father's favor from him and destroyed it. Then the garments that were tokens of Potiphar's favor were taken from Joseph and used to falsely accuse him and get him placed in prison. But when he ascended to power in Pharaoh's house, he was once again given fine linens to wear. This time those garments were not taken from him. Even if the Enemy, other people, or life's circumstances take your coat, don't you worry—He can replace the coat.

JOURNAL DAY 6

1. Will I allow God to bring about maturity in me, even if it is accomplished through hardship?

2. Can I be trusted by God to serve those who have harmed me in the past, if He calls me to do so?

3. List times in your life when God supernaturally placed you in positions in which you could not have placed yourself.

Devotional Day 7:

MOST HIGH GOD

⁶ Now there was a day when the sons of God came to present themselves before the Lord, and Satan also came among them. ⁷ And the Lord said to Satan, "From where do you come?"

So Satan answered the Lord and said, "From going to and fro on the earth, and from walking back and forth on it."

⁸ Then the Lord said to Satan, "Have you considered My servant Job, that there is none like him on the earth, a blameless and upright man, one who fears God and shuns evil?"

⁹ So Satan answered the Lord and said, "Does Job fear God for nothing? ¹⁰ Have You not made a hedge around him, around his household, and around all that he has on every side? You have blessed the work of his hands, and his possessions have increased in the land. ¹¹ But now, stretch out Your hand and touch all that he has, and he will surely curse You to Your face!"

¹² And the Lord said to Satan, "Behold, all that he has is in your power; only do not lay a hand on his person."

So Satan went out from the presence of the Lord (NKJV).

The book of Job is a 42 chapter account of the life of Job, someone the Scriptures describe as "blameless and upright" and one who feared the Lord and put away evil. Job had 10 children, an abundance of possessions, and was considered to be a great man. The Scriptures describe how Job would regularly get up early in the morning and make offerings on behalf of his children's sins.

Satan went to the Lord, and the Lord asked him where he had been. Satan responded that he had been walking back and forth on the earth. Then the Lord asked Satan if he had considered Job and described him the way the Scriptures introduced him, as blameless and upright. The Lord set Job apart from others in His conversation with Satan by stating that there was "none like him on the earth."

Satan pushed back and attached Job's character to his current positive environment. He claimed Job was faithful because of the hedge God had placed around him and because God had so bountifully blessed him. The Lord then gave Satan power over all that Job had but restricted him from touching Job's person.

Then Job lost everything.

He lost his oxen and donkeys to the Sabeans, who also killed the servants who worked there. While Job was being told that news, another messenger reported that fire came from heaven and consumed the sheep and the servants with them. While that report was being given to him, another messenger told him of the Chaldeans, how they took the camels and killed the servants. Finally, while he was being told of the Chaldeans, another messenger came and told him that a wind came and knocked the house down on his children, causing them all to perish.

Let's read Job's initial and immediate response to this unimaginable tragedy in Job 1:20–22:

> *20 Then Job arose, tore his robe, and shaved his head; and he fell to the ground and worshiped.*
> *21 And he said:*
>
> *"Naked I came from my mother's womb,*
>
> *And naked shall I return there.*
>
> *The Lord gave, and the Lord has taken away;*
>
> *Blessed be the name of the Lord."*
>
> *22 In all this Job did not sin nor charge God with wrong (NKJV).*

Job lost everything. The resources by which he built his wealth, and his family were stripped from him. Even more, *all of his children were killed in an instant.*

But he did not curse God.

For several years, I struggled with the story of Job. I could barely stand to read the text. I could understand how a person can lose material possessions, be reduced to nothing financially, and still have peace. What I could not understand was the loss of Job's children. I cannot even fathom the pain of losing, in an instant, 10 (or any number) of children.

One of the most difficult clauses I have read in the Bible is found at the beginning of Job 1:8: "Then the Lord said to Satan…"

Satan did not ask the Lord about Job. In fact, Satan did not ask the Lord about anyone. God brought up Job in a seemingly unprompted manner and then gave Satan permission to do what he would with all that Job had.

For years, as I either experienced or witnessed others experiencing serial and concurrent tragedies and traumas, I skipped the book of Job as my Bible study text because I simply could not rationalize why a loving God would place someone He describes as "blameless and upright" in harm's way. I just did not understand.

And you know what? I still don't understand.

I remember meeting with a potential client one day and fighting back tears in the office as I listened to her describe losing two of her three adult children years apart. She was calm as she spoke, but I noticed a sadness in her eyes as soon as I shook her hand before our appointment. She was kind, thoughtful, accomplished, and quite polished. She had an authority, a self-assurance in the way she spoke, but it was quieter now. I imagine that voice used to sound different.

She wasn't crying as she told me, so I knew I could not either. But my soul cried for her. I kept thinking, *"Why?"*

Why does she have to go on the rest of her life like this? What about her child she still has? What is he supposed to do?

She indicated that her children's father was not around, so I had no way of knowing if she had any support system. As she spoke, I prayed for her. I asked God to help me keep the tears at bay. I wished there was something I could do, but there was not.

The book of Job came to mind then, but I did not read it.

There was another mother I found out about whose son had a tragic accident and initially survived. His parents, family, community, and people all over the world prayed, interceded, and supported in the ways that they could. I watched his mother's strength rise up in a way that moved me, convicted me, challenged me, and inspired me.

He began to make progress. It was a miracle! I spoke his name before God daily, "Lord, heal this baby. I know You will." I was confident—excited even that the world would see this miracle unfold and know it was the Lord's doing.

And then he died.

When I read the statement made by his mother, the room started to spin. I felt dizzy and nauseous. I was in a state of total disbelief. We were specific in our prayers. God please heal him on this side of heaven so we can have him here with us. We were consistent. We were persistent. And God took him home.

In the days, weeks, and months that followed, I witnessed a mother give God glory anyway. She was not dishonest about her broken heart. She did not sanitize her descriptions of her feelings or paint an untrue picture. She told the truth about how she felt, how her husband felt, how her other children felt. In all of that, she still gave God glory.

The book of Job came to mind then too—but I still did not read it.

It simply did not seem like the place in the Bible to go when your heart is already in so much pain.

At some point, the Holy Spirit began to work on my heart when it came to reading the book of Job. Here and there I would read bits and pieces of it for as long as I could stand it. It seemed like every tragic and unfair scenario would come to my mind as I would read. Then the Lord helped to shift my perspective. I moved my focus from the magnitude of Job's suffering to the magnitude of God. He is bigger than all the tragedies. He is Lord; the situation and circumstance are not.

I have heard that God is Sovereign all my life. I realized, though, that my idea of His sovereignty was limited to this: my God can do all things. That is true—He can. But sometimes He doesn't do the thing that I want or that I think would be best for the person in the situation.

What I have come to accept and find comfort in is the true sovereignty of God. I have learned to appreciate that God is not so small that I can explain everything about Him, or co-sign all His decisions, or intellectualize His grandeur. That means that even what He does not do is a part of His plan. I have learned to rest on this truth in God's Word: *His thoughts and ways are truly higher than ours (see Isaiah 55:8–9).*

God knows why He mentioned Job to Satan. He knows why He allowed such suffering to befall Job. He knows why He allowed the suffering to last for as long as it did and why He chose to stop it when He did. He is the Most High God. He is intentional. He is consistent. He makes no mistakes. And since God is omniscient (all-knowing), I do not have to be.

Read that last sentence again—but slower.

We often worry and are anxious when our Father knows *everything*.

He tells us in His Word that He knows the plans He has for us. Those plans are to prosper, not to harm us (see Jeremiah 29:11). So, I can lean on the completeness of God and the fact that He lacks nothing. That means I, as His child, also lack nothing.

> # HIS THOUGHTS AND WAYS ARE TRULY HIGHER THAN OURS.

There is trouble I have both experienced myself and witnessed in others' lives for which I still have no explanation. And while I could never comprehend the volume and density of the love the Lord has for me; I know He loves me so much. There are experiences I have had that

I am still not happy about, but I have come to be grateful that God trusts me with trials. I have learned to rejoice, not that I am in the trial, but that He knows I will bless His Name through it. He will not leave me in it alone.

JOURNAL DAY 7

1. Recall some experiences that you still may not understand, but you would like the Lord to help you accept His sovereignty over.

2. Today is the end of week one of the Daniel Fast. How is my life and spiritual walk different than it was a week ago?

THINGS TOO WONDERFUL

[1] Then Job answered the Lord and said:

[2] "I know that You can do everything,

And that no purpose of Yours can be withheld from You.

[3] You asked, 'Who is this who hides counsel without knowledge?'

Therefore I have uttered what I did not understand,

Things too wonderful for me, which I did not know.

[4] Listen, please, and let me speak;

You said, 'I will question you, and you shall answer Me.'

[5] "I have heard of You by the hearing of the ear,

But now my eye sees You.

[6] Therefore I abhor myself,

And repent in dust and ashes" (NKJV).

After Job lost his possessions and his children, Satan approached the Lord again. The Lord asked him where he had been, and he responded that he had been walking back and forth on the earth. Then the Lord brings up Job again. He asks Satan if he had considered Job and describes him as "blameless and upright," just as before. The Lord says of Job in chapter 2, verse 3, "And he holds fast to his integrity, although you incited Me against him, to destroy him without cause" (NKJV).

Satan's rebuttal was that if he could touch Job's person, then Job would curse God to His face. The Lord gave him permission to attack Job's health, but he was not permitted to take Job's life. Satan caused Job to be covered with boils. His wife, at the depths of Job's suffering, told him to "curse God and die" (Job 2:9 NKJV).

As the suffering became extended, Job had some questions for the Lord while he despaired. The book of Job contains chapters filled with Job's words and the words of his three friends who came to him—it also includes some accusations of Job and some questions.

The questions Job had for the Lord may seem like a natural response to such sudden and extended suffering. He had experienced loss and devastation too great for many of us to even imagine. God answers Job in an unexpected way. He responds with questions of His own for Job:

¹ Then the Lord answered Job out of the whirlwind, and said:

² "Who is this who darkens counsel

By words without knowledge?

³ Now prepare yourself like a man;

I will question you, and you shall answer Me.

⁴ "Where were you when I laid the foundations of the earth?

Tell Me, if you have understanding.

⁵ Who determined its measurements?"

Surely you know! (Job 38:1–5 NKJV).

The questions continue for several verses and across chapters. They reflect a beautiful account of God's boundless ability, His wisdom, His sovereignty, and His ever presence. Each line in the passage is a testament from the mouth of the Lord. It is awe-inspiring and perfect.

This was another part of the book of Job that was difficult for me to read for many years. However, it reveals a critical principle for navigating hardship and suffering: *We must trust an All-Sufficient God over a sufficient explanation.*

When Job posed questions to God, the Lord could have responded with an explanation of Job's circumstances. He could have responded by telling Job that his story would end in restoration and a double blessing. He could have looked inside the heart of Job, saw what Job wanted to hear, and spoken words of reassurance and encouragement that aligned with what Job wanted.

Instead, God responded with questions that illustrated the infiniteness of His power, knowledge, and holiness. Maybe He did that because it is more important that we trust the character of God than the logic of man.

The first question that comes to my mind when I hear about a horrific event or experience betrayal, or loss is *"Why?"*

Why would that person take an innocent life?

Why would they hurt a child?

Why do they hold so much hatred in their heart?

Why did that person have to die so soon?

The likelihood is that there is no explanation that would allow me to accept such an enormous loss. So, even if an answer was given, it would not be sufficient. There are traumas that cannot be rationalized, explained, or reasoned. When I recall some of my most painful memories—some of the most traumatic events in my life—it is true every time. There is no explanation that would make me say, "Okay, that's fine now."

But God is All-Sufficient. He says in 2 Corinthians 12:9, "My grace is sufficient for you, for My strength is made perfect in weakness" (NKJV).

I don't know what your Job situation is or was. But God knows, and He is trustworthy. Anything He has not extended to you is not because He wants to harm you. Rather, He knows your needs better than you know your own.

WE MUST TRUST AN ALL-SUFFICIENT GOD OVER A SUFFICIENT EXPLANATION.

Sometimes, I will pray for people as they are hurting or suffering. I can sometimes become almost frantic in my pleading on their behalf. God always reminds me, *"I love them more than you do."* The revelation washes over me every time. He's right. As much as I feel that I love some people, it is no match for His love for us. He sent His Son to *die*. For me. For you. That was His choice. He could have made any choice He wanted.

Understand that His hand was not forced. He was not coerced. His love is not contrived. He chose us. He continues to choose us all the time.

After God completes His questioning of Job, in Job 42:1–6, Job repents. He acknowledges his human limitation and his finite mind. He describes the things of God as "things too wonderful, which I did not know" (Job 42:3 NKJV).

There is a space that can come when we accept what God allows. When we decide we believe that which is already true about God—that He is good, perfect, unchanging, and unfailing—we can remove the need to understand everything in our lives.

I recall a time in my life where there was a professional assignment I wanted to take. I had done it before and benefited greatly from it. My life had improved personally, professionally, and financially. I was convinced that this same type of assignment was again the answer for my advancement and wellness.

I applied and was immediately received favorably. All the feedback I was receiving made it seem like I was being called to the assignment. I even purchased the gear and tools I would need to accompany me. I had my mind set that this was mine, and I simply needed to walk into it.

Then everything came to a halt. All the approvals began to be rescinded. Words were retracted. The assignment was canceled.

I thought that because God had used it before, He would use the same thing again. But that was not so. While the loss of this assignment was not traumatic, I was internally mourning the missed opportunity to escape the actual trauma I was experiencing.

I had so many questions for God. Why let me think that I had it and then take it away? How was I going to cope with the trauma I so desperately wanted to escape? How was I going to progress financially, physically, emotionally, and spiritually?

The Lord let me know that He is in control. He is the Beginning and the End. The way He answered my questions was not what I wanted. He did not tell me why He blocked the assignment. They denied me several times, no matter which direction I approached applying. He did not foretell of a double blessing.

I had to accept that His reasoning—His plan—was just too wonderful for me to understand. It sparked a series of events once I accepted that last denial as final in my heart. God began to move in ways that, had I taken that assignment, He would not have moved. Over time, He revealed that what He had for me instead was double, triple, quadruple what I would have gained from the assignment I thought I wanted. Even years later, I see that the return from what God did have in mind is now exponential. Granting me that initial assignment would not have been the loving thing for my Father to do.

The time between being denied and experiencing God's preferred blessing felt excruciating. One of the hardest parts was obeying God in turning down one of the ways I could have gotten what I wanted. I heard Him say, "No." I had a choice. I was obedient, but I was not thrilled about it. I felt like I was giving up a sure thing, something I knew well and had experienced before, for a list of unknowns.

That is precisely why we need to see God as Lord of our lives and not our circumstances. If I look to my environment for deliverance, I will end up being let down. If I look to material or earthly things to sustain me, I will fall apart. But if I look to God to be my Foundation and my Source, He will be so much more sufficient than an assignment, an explanation, or an answer.

We know we are growing when we can ask God a question, not get the answer we want, and still trust Him. The growth for me did not occur when God blessed me later with much more. The growth occurred when I turned down the assignment and trusted Him to be the One who meets my needs before I know what He is about to do in my life.

It was how I waited that showed the position of my heart. To the questions you have, He is the Answer. And He is faithful in perpetuity, so you can rest in Him.

JOURNAL DAY 8

1.   Can I accept a situation God allowed, even when He offers no explanation for why He allowed it?

2.   In what areas can I relinquish control to the Lord—therefore casting my burden onto Him?

THE LIFTER OF MY HEAD

¹⁰ And the Lord restored Job's losses when he prayed for his friends. Indeed the Lord gave Job twice as much as he had before. ¹¹ Then all his brothers, all his sisters, and all those who had been his acquaintances before, came to him and ate food with him in his house; and they consoled him and comforted him for all the adversity that the Lord had brought upon him. Each one gave him a piece of silver and each a ring of gold.

¹² Now the Lord blessed the latter days of Job more than his beginning; for he had fourteen thousand sheep, six thousand camels, one thousand yoke of oxen, and one thousand female donkeys. ¹³ He also had seven sons and three daughters. ¹⁴ And he called the name of the first Jemimah, the name of the second Keziah, and the name of the third Keren-Happuch. ¹⁵ In all the land were found no women so beautiful as the daughters of Job; and their father gave them an inheritance among their brothers.

¹⁶ After this Job lived one hundred and forty years, and saw his children and grandchildren for four generations. ¹⁷ So Job died, old and full of days (NKJV).

Following Job's repentance, the Lord still had a request of Job. It was critical that he was still obedient—even following such a long period of suffering. The Lord spoke to one of Job's three friends, Eliphaz, and expressed His anger toward them. He said, "My wrath is aroused against you and your two friends, for you have not spoken of Me what is right, as My servant Job has. Now therefore, take for yourselves seven bulls and seven rams, go to My servant Job, and offer up for yourselves a burnt offering; and My servant Job shall pray for you. For I will accept him, lest I deal with you according to your folly; because you have not spoken of Me what is right, as My servant Job has" (Job 42:7–8 NKJV).

Job had been pressed unto his breaking point, and the same friends who at times in his journey spoke against him, God told Job to pray for. Job 42:10 says that Job was restored when he obeyed and prayed for his friends. His obedience is what God responded to with restoration. And when God restored him, He blessed him twice what he had lost. Job lived to see four generations of his children and grandchildren, and he died in old age.

The conclusion of the book of Job leaves us with this truth of God: *He will meet all our needs and redeem that which was lost.*

We should be careful though, to heed the voice of God, because some blessings He releases are a response. He is looking for our obedience, so it is clear that we seek to please Him and not ourselves.

The restoration of Job is beautiful and miraculous. But as I noted in Day 7 of our devotional journey, I always thought about how Job being blessed with more children did not bring back the children who died. Yes, the material possessions can be replaced in a way that feels equivalent, but people are unique—each with their own personalities and values.

This story of restoration also brings to my mind Naomi, who was Ruth's mother-in-law. Naomi's husband, Elimelech, died. Then her two sons, Mahlon and Chilion (who married Moabites: Orpah and Ruth), also passed away. She tried to send her daughters-in-law back to their land since she had no other sons. Orpah turned back, but Ruth remained.

When Ruth and Naomi arrived in Bethlehem, the women called Naomi by her name, but she replied, "Do not call me Naomi; call me Mara, for the Almighty has dealt very bitterly with me" (Ruth 1:20 ESV).

Curious, I looked up what the name Naomi means. It is a Hebrew name that means 'pleasant' or 'pleasantness.' Naomi was in so much pain that she could not even bear to be called by the name of her birth because her life was not a reflection of that name. The name Mara means 'bitter.' So she felt that was a more accurate depiction of her plight.

The story of Ruth and Naomi is another beautiful story of restoration and redemption. A man named Boaz married Ruth, thereby redeeming Naomi's family lineage. Boaz and Ruth had a son named Obed, the father of Jesse, the father of David. God used a painful story of loss and turned it into something glorious.

The Scriptures do not tell us what Naomi was thinking at the end of the book of Ruth, but I imagine she still loved and missed the husband and sons she lost. I imagine the same for Job and the 10 children he lost. Naomi's grandson, Obed, and Job's seven sons and three daughters likely brought them each so much joy. I think that joy sometimes coexists with the grief of who or what was before.

> **HE WILL MEET ALL OUR NEEDS AND REDEEM THAT WHICH WAS LOST.**

God does not always meet our needs the way we want Him to, but He will always meet them. Sometimes that will mean existing in a space of pain and peace, joy and sorrow, gratitude and weariness.

Have you ever really wanted something done that you knew only God could do? Maybe you prayed and prayed over it. So many times, God has answered my prayers and responded with "Yes." Sometimes, though, the answer was "No." Sometimes, it was "Wait." I can think of a few things that I have prayed for over several years. I am still waiting. He is a Good Father. So when He tells me "No," I must interpret that to mean this request I think I need is not truly a need. And if He wants me to wait, I can trust there is a purpose in the waiting period.

Several years ago, I went through a season of great sadness. I felt exhausted, unmotivated, and despondent. Simple tasks were disproportionately difficult, and a sense of hopelessness lingered over me. I often thought to myself, *this can't be it. This can't be all there is.* I consistently felt like I was not accomplishing enough, was not moving fast enough, and was not covering enough ground. I had this need for success and achievement. It was the only thing that gave me temporary relief from my depressed state.

Much later, I realized that what I yearned for was the purpose of God for my life. What I thought I needed at the time, though, was a counterfeit—earthly success. I had a deeply rooted desire to prove my naysayers wrong, to beat the odds, and to show that I was not what some people had said I was. However, I would experience accomplishment after accomplishment, victory after victory, and it was not enough. I thought I would try law school. At another point, medical school. I kept asking God, "What do you want me to do?" I felt like I was wandering through life, trying to reach a goal post that kept moving as soon as I neared it.

I had a misunderstanding of what true fulfillment was and was misinformed about my purpose. When I discovered the purpose of my life is to worship Him, then I began to come out of that season of sadness. It's that simple. That means that whatever I do, I should do it to bring God glory (see Colossians 3:23). The specific role I hold at the time is not nearly as consequential. The second wave of revelation that God used to deliver me out of that season was to let me know He would guide my path.

What I did not realize before was that He often guides us step-by-step. I was frustrated because I did not have the full layout of the next several years already in mind. That was by design. He wants to guide us in increments, using each step as a space of development, deepened relationship, and greater reliance on Him. If He had told me all that He would eventually do through me, I would have either relied on the plan instead of the Planner, shrunk back in fear at the impossibility of it all, or some other variation of having my eye on something aside from Him.

He did not allow that season because He wanted to hurt me. He allowed it so I could see the difference between attempting to create my own joy and peace and allowing the Prince of Peace to be my peace.

A description of God that I love so much is in Psalm 3:3: "But you, O Lord, are a shield about me, my glory, and the lifter of my head" (ESV).

He is the lifter of my head. Just reading that statement makes me sit up a little straighter, walk a little taller, and smile much wider.

There is a purpose to everything God does and everything He allows. We cannot always perceive the purpose. We can, however, stand in faith on the fact that God knows our needs better than we do. He cannot fail, and He is the Restorer. In His omnipotence, He can even restore time to us. Joel 2:25 says, "And I will restore to you the years that the locust hath eaten, the cankerworm, and the caterpillar, and the palmerworm, my great army which I sent among you" (KJV).

The restoration of God is not always a one-to-one tradeoff the way we might imagine. But He can do more with less time. He can bring one opportunity that restores the loss of many others. He can bring a relationship that is a space of respite in a way that makes up for several hurtful ones previously. He's God like that.

God never makes a promise that He will not keep. There will be concepts about the Lord that will be, as they were for Job, too wonderful for us to understand.

Incomprehensible. Matchless. Most High God.

In chapter 1, there was reference to a name of God called "Jehovah Jireh." It means, 'The Lord will provide.' Even in seasons of great loss, He will provide. The word "will" in the definition of that name of God represents a perpetual provision from God. It indicates that He is Provision. We can seek Him about anything and everything, and He always has what we need.

That is the kind of God upon which we can build a foundation of faith that will not be blown away by adversity.

I still do not enjoy reading about Job's misfortune, and It still breaks my heart to imagine his affliction and agony. I would not wish that even on an enemy. But a shift in perspective has helped me as I read. However massive and cavernous the pit of suffering is—however intense and confining the area—however isolating and depressing the condition—God is bigger. He is undefeated. He can make all things new.

1.   Have I allowed Him lordship over all the areas of my life, especially those where I feel the most insecure?

2.   Do I believe He is who He says He is—Jehovah Jireh and my Redeemer?

Devotional Day 10:

PECULIAR METHODS

¹⁵ Now on the day that the tabernacle was raised up, the cloud covered the tabernacle, the tent of the Testimony; from evening until morning it was above the tabernacle like the appearance of fire. ¹⁶ So it was always: the cloud covered it by day, and the appearance of fire by night. ¹⁷ Whenever the cloud was taken up from above the tabernacle, after that the children of Israel would journey; and in the place where the cloud settled, there the children of Israel would pitch their tents. ¹⁸ At the command of the Lord the children of Israel would journey, and at the command of the Lord they would camp; as long as the cloud stayed above the tabernacle they remained encamped. ¹⁹ Even when the cloud continued long, many days above the tabernacle, the children of Israel kept the charge of the Lord and did not journey. ²⁰ So it was, when the cloud was above the tabernacle a few days: according to the command of the Lord they would remain encamped, and according to the command of the Lord they would journey (NKJV).

After the Lord brought His people, the Israelites, out of captivity in Egypt, He led them along their path in a particular way. By day, He used a cloud and by night, a pillar of fire. The Israelites spent many generations in slavery in Egypt, and most likely many of them spent their lives as slaves. In the book of Exodus, we see the Lord also using the cloud and pillar of fire to lead the Israelites out of Egypt to the Red Sea, where He defeated Pharaoh and his army and brought His children across on dry land.

The text does not mention that God spoke through the cloud or the fire. It does not state that the Israelites were given any sneak peek of the step after the current one or a clue as to how long a step would be. They did, however, see the victory of the Lord at the Red Sea and His mighty deliverance. The Egyptian Pharaoh, their oppressor for so many years, was wiped out with his army all at once. Just like that.

In our modern cultural context, it is difficult to imagine being led by something that did not speak audibly or offer any secondary, external confirmation that it was moving the "right" way, or that was inanimate and not personal or human in nature.

Sometimes, though, is that not a parallel to how God leads us?

Most of us have never heard His audible voice, and His guidance can feel to us like pieces are "missing." Maybe He tells us when to do something but not why. Maybe He tells us to move, but not what the ultimate destination is. Maybe He says to pray, but does not reveal to us if our prayer will be answered the way we want.

The account of the Israelites being guided by the cloud and pillar of fire is a picture of how God still wants to guide us. *He wants us to know that we can trust His character and nature—even when His methods seem strange.*

God knows the end from the beginning (see Isaiah 46:10). So, it is good for us not to limit Him in our minds to only being God in certain ways and using certain methods.

He can use a cloud or fire to guide our path. He can use a donkey to speak to a man (see Numbers 22:28). He can bring water from a rock to quench His people's thirst (see Exodus 17:6). He can make mud from dirt and spit and use it to restore a man's sight (see John 9:6–7).

We are thousands of years removed from such accounts, so maybe they don't feel as relatable.

For you, He might use your three-year-old to say something they could not have known yet aside from Him. He could cause a delay that is inconvenient at the time, but proves to be beneficial in a way you could not have predicted. He could tell you to move, to stay, to be quiet, to speak up, to take the job, to leave the industry, or to apologize. Any of these could feel completely counterintuitive, uncomfortable, or contrary to your preferences or thoughts on how things should go.

This is where it is critical to trust the character of God.

His character is Victor. He showed the Israelites this at the Red Sea. His character is Finisher. He brought the Israelites out of Egypt and then removed the possibility of them being taken captive again by their oppressor. His character is Good Father. When He tells us to do something, when He leads us a certain way or uses a certain method, it is because He knows the outcome. That outcome is for our good and His glory.

HE WANTS US TO KNOW THAT WE CAN TRUST HIS CHARACTER AND NATURE.

When God leads me using a peculiar method, I remember the Lord leading the Israelites by a cloud and a pillar of fire, and I remember Joshua and the Battle of Jericho.

Joshua chapter 6 described this battle that did not seem like a battle at all. The Lord told Joshua He would deliver Jericho to him. Jericho was a well-fortified city with impenetrable walls. The method of deliverance was not to prepare for an intense and bloody battle. It was not to develop and send their most skilled fighters. It was for the army to march around the city once each day for six days, with seven priests carrying horns. On the seventh day, the army was to march around the city seven times, while the priests blew the trumpets.

Then they were to shout, and the walls would fall.

When I feel like I am facing a monumental adversary or obstacle, I am inclined to take even more monumental action to defeat it. I tend to feel like I need to take huge steps or deliver detrimental blows to make a difference in my circumstance. So, while I much enjoy the song about it, the Battle of Jericho would have likely been a difficult one for me to fight.

My natural leaning is to bring the tool for the task at hand. That is not bad advice, but God sometimes wants us to trust Him over the tool or the plan we may have.

One year, I had hit a milestone financially that I never could have imagined attaining. Every time I reflected on the years I spent in lack, I would be brought to tears and washed in gratitude. I was poised to achieve some more milestones the next year because of what that initial year had produced. Expectant, I would excitedly whisper to God from time to time how He was the Great Multiplier and how He turned my life around in every way, to include the area of finances.

In a savings account, I had the largest sum on hand than I had ever managed to accumulate in my life. I had big plans for those funds—plans I thought were consistent with the way He had instructed me to conduct myself financially.

One day, He said something strange.

He put a number, a dollar amount in my mind that was bigger than the number in my whole savings account. I waited. He gave me the name of a church in a different city and state that I had never attended. I had only ever watched online. He said, "Give that amount of money in the year-end offering at that church."

I had to sit down.

I had responsibilities. I had debts *He* told me to pay. I had rental properties; if something went wrong, I had to pay. That number was even bigger than the largest amount of money I had ever managed to pay. The bills would still be due. He had instructed me to never borrow money for anything for the rest of my life. So, if I ran out of money, I could not ask for help. I am not someone who is comfortable asking for help, anyway. I was confused.

Why would He tell me to give away the very resource that was helping me to obey Him in giving and in stewardship? By the way, this church *had* money! They weren't hurting for it at all!

Then it struck me in the center of my chest. The same God who enabled me to save this sum up—the same God who permitted the financial success—the same God who was completely aware of all the responsibilities with which He had entrusted me—was now trusting me with something greater.

It had been a while since I experienced financial lack. And though I remember it well, there was still space between me and it. This was the test. Who did I trust? Did I trust my ability to work and produce? Did I trust the resource of finances? Or did I trust God?

I booked my flight, rental car, and room for the weekend. Days before I left, He provided just enough for me to give nearly all I had in the year-end offering at the church He specified. He gave me boldness as I traveled. He showed Himself in the airport, in parking lots, at the church, at the rental car desk—He showed up everywhere.

He saved me a seat in the sanctuary. He delivered a word through the pastor just for me, and He sat me next to people who would pour into and be a blessing to me. By the time I dropped the check in the offering box, I was overwhelmed with gratitude that He would ask that of me. I knew He couldn't ask that of everyone.

The Bible says in Luke 6:38, "Give, and it will be given to you. A good measure, pressed down, shaken together, and running over, will be poured into your lap. For with the measure you use, it will be measured to you" (NIV).

It was counterintuitive to give it all away when I owed so much and had so much responsibility. But God used this peculiar method to create a testimony in me. I did not give to receive—but the Lord will fulfill His Word always. Miraculously, He restored me and then some in a matter of days, not months.

I tell this story to encourage you. When His methods seem strange, you can still trust Him. He loves to work in ways that make it clear that He is the Author. He is the same God at Jericho, the same God who sent the cloud and the fire, and the same God who showed up at the airport and in the church. He gave the victory in each scenario because that is who He is—The Victorious One.

1.   Have I confined God to a box of how I think He must operate, or am I open to that which may seem strange to me?

2.   Will you give your all in any way He directs, to be obedient and submitted to Him?

Devotional Day 11:

THEY THAT WAIT

²¹ Then Moses stretched out his hand over the sea, and all that night the Lord drove the sea back with a strong east wind and turned it into dry land. The waters were divided, ²² and the Israelites went through the sea on dry ground, with a wall of water on their right and on their left.

²³ The Egyptians pursued them, and all Pharaoh's horses and chariots and horsemen followed them into the sea. ²⁴ During the last watch of the night the Lord looked down from the pillar of fire and cloud at the Egyptian army and threw it into confusion. ²⁵ He jammed the wheels of their chariots so that they had difficulty driving. And the Egyptians said, "Let's get away from the Israelites! The Lord is fighting for them against Egypt."

²⁶ Then the Lord said to Moses, "Stretch out your hand over the sea so that the waters may flow back over the Egyptians and their chariots and horsemen." ²⁷ Moses stretched out his hand over the sea, and at daybreak the sea went back to its place. The Egyptians were fleeing toward it, and the Lord swept them into the sea. ²⁸ The water flowed back and covered the chariots and horsemen—the entire army of Pharaoh that had followed the Israelites into the sea. Not one of them survived (NIV).

As a child, when I would hear about the story of the crossing of the Red Sea, I missed a consequential phrase, "all that night." When Moses stretched his hand out over the Red Sea, it did not immediately part, and the land become dry. That's how I used to imagine it. Moses' hand went up, the waters parted, the Israelites skipped on through, and the water came back down. That was not an accurate reading of the story. God used the wind as a process by which to part the sea *overnight*.

God led the Israelites into an impossible place. They would either drown in the sea or be slaughtered by their enemy. Waiting for the sea to be parted overnight, as they were being hunted down by Pharaoh's army, could not have been a comfortable experience. Exodus 14:19–20 is such a poignant example of how God works in our wait. It says, "And the Angel of God, who went before the camp of Israel, moved, and went behind them; and the pillar of cloud went from before them and stood behind them. So it came between the camp of the Egyptians and the camp of Israel. Thus it was a cloud and darkness to the one, and it gave light by night to the other, so that the one did not come near the other all that night" (NKJV).

The Egyptians were right behind the Israelites, but God blocked their access to them while He solved the issue. The Scriptures do not indicate that the Lord told Moses or the people that it would take a night to push back the seas. So, they had to wait for God to complete it when He would.

The process of waiting, by itself, can be challenging. It can be more challenging when the wait is for an unknown period of time. When there is no hint or way to calculate the duration. Waiting on the Lord is different from simply waiting in the natural; *Waiting on the Lord is a place and position of renewal, even in an emergency.* The Bible says in Isaiah 40:31:

"But those who wait on the Lord

Shall renew their strength;

They shall mount up with wings like eagles,

They shall run and not be weary,

They shall walk and not faint" (NKJV).

There is so much joy to experience in the reading of this passage. This tells us that waiting on the Lord, instead of being an exhausting, draining, and sorrowful time, is intended to be a space where we actually *derive* strength in the Lord. It is where we can be encouraged and hopeful in Him.

As the Israelites waited for their next step to be revealed, they could rest in the character of the God who delivered them. That same, unchanging God would not cease to be Deliverer in the next season. He does not change!

> **WAITING ON THE LORD IS A PLACE AND POSITION OF RENEWAL.**

He does not waste our waiting either. He is always developing, transforming, speaking, and moving during those times.

There are accounts in the Bible for long waits like the time Abraham and Sarah had to wait before having a son. Or like the time Noah had to wait for the ark to be completed and the rains to come. Those require a spiritual endurance not easily developed.

When you are in an impossible situation where both directions look futile, waiting any amount of time can seem too long. The level of desperation intensifies the need for a breakthrough or a solution.

At the Red Sea, the oppressor of the Israelites was after them. They were being actively pursued by those who wished to kill them. This was an emergency.

When Moses' mother put him in a basket in the river to save him from being killed in accordance with Pharaoh's decree to throw all the Hebrew baby boys into the river, the wait until Pharaoh's daughter retrieved her son probably felt endless (see Exodus 2).

Sometimes we wait for health test results, or school acceptance letters, or adoption confirmation. Maybe the length of time is not several years, but it is critical. That time feels multiplied.

Years ago, just before my last quarter of grad school, I encountered a problem I had not faced before. My grades had fallen 0.001 points below the required minimum GPA, and they kicked me out of school.

Over the years, I had consistently done well academically. However, the outside pressures mounted while I was in grad school. So much was working against the direction in which I was moving. My best efforts were not yielding the results I was accustomed to producing.

When I received the letter from the University, I froze. This degree was more than a piece of paper to me. It represented the means by which I would secure employment with higher compensation so I could provide for myself and those the Lord had assigned to me. It represented an escape from lack and the start of a new, better season. One more quarter was all I needed to graduate.

The letter stated I could appeal the decision within a certain number of days. I had a short time frame before the final quarter started, and I drafted a letter requesting readmission to the program. The wait for the response could not have been more than a few days, but it felt much longer. There was so much depending on my completion of the degree.

I asked the Lord to give me unreasonable favor in the eyes of the board. I asked him to remove obstacles that would impede my progress and grant me grace. And I waited.

As time went on, I expected the waiting to get worse. But something I did not anticipate happened. I felt stronger the longer I waited. As I spent time with the Lord, He ministered to me, and He spoke to me about the areas in my life that led to my dismissal. He was not accusatory or cold. He was loving. He was holding me accountable in the way that I would imagine a loving father would hold his child accountable. He was firm but compassionate and showed me how I had allowed my legitimate obstacles to cause me to make illegitimate excuses internally.

Although I never voiced these excuses, they still affected my movements and motivation. The Lord wanted to develop in me long-suffering. That was a word I remembered reading in the Bible, but to which I paid little attention. During that season, I learned that long-suffering was one of the fruits of the Spirit (see Galatians 5:22). It is a word that means patience and the ability to withstand trouble over time.

God wanted me to have the ability to experience trouble and not become bitter, angry, or filled with excuses. He wanted me to learn to hide in Him and bring Him everything—the large and the small. He wanted me to remain grateful in adversity, not entitled or obstinate. This humbling experience that He allowed drew me to the only One who could help me.

When the letter came in the mail with the response, my hand shook just a little. I started to think about what I would do with my life if I had ruined this chance to improve it. Then I remembered God had the final say and that He always means me well. So, the outcome was not important as long as He was with me. Even if it did not go my way, it would have been because He had another, better way to get me to the destination He had in mind.

My hand stopped trembling. I opened the letter deliberately and with confidence in the Lord. I pulled out a single sheet of paper and gave my eyes a second to focus.

I was relieved to see that they readmitted me. God had been gracious to me.

I ended my last quarter strong and graduated ahead of time—finishing the whole two-year program in a total of one year.

He did not just restore me; He accelerated me. I have never forgotten His mercy in that and so many other seasons.

And He removed any shame I would have felt without Him.

Everything He does, He does to completion. So even if you are not called to move in an area at the time, trust that He is still working, and that His methods are steadfast and infallible.

1.   How can I shift my perspective on waiting to reflect more closely what the Scripture says in Isaiah 40?

2.   List some of the positive things that have come out of times of waiting.

3.   Reflect on the parts of your character God developed in you when you waited on Him.

Devotional Day 12:

ON HIS MARK

Genesis 21:1–5

¹ Now the Lord was gracious to Sarah as he had said, and the Lord did for Sarah what he had promised. ² Sarah became pregnant and bore a son to Abraham in his old age, at the very time God had promised him. ³ Abraham gave the name Isaac to the son Sarah bore him. ⁴ When his son Isaac was eight days old, Abraham circumcised him, as God commanded him. ⁵ Abraham was a hundred years old when his son Isaac was born to him (NIV).

A hundred years old seems a little late to be having a baby. Abraham waited a lifetime for his namesake to come to pass. Abraham means 'father of nations' or 'father of multitudes.' Even his previous name, Abram, means 'exalted father.' So his name said something about him that was not true for a very long time. God knew his future though, even when Abraham could not see it.

When God says something, it is true right then, even if we do not see the evidence of it in the natural. However, knowing that does not always make it easier for us to wait on the promise, since our view is so limited. It takes an intentional strengthening of our faith to have the ability to wait well and not take matters into our own hands.

God kept his promise to Abraham and Sarah, but we see the result of doubting the Lord when Sarah (at the time called "Sarai") told her husband to sleep with her maidservant Hagar so he could have a child, since she had not conceived yet herself. The child born as the result of that union was Ishmael. His birth was accompanied by the kind of consequences that come with moving outside of God's will.

Later, the son who was promised to Abraham and Sarah, Isaac, was born. The Lord was gracious to keep His covenant with Abraham, even though Abraham and his wife had failed to wait well on the Lord. Abraham's story and the fulfillment of the promise shows us this: *God stands outside of time, and His timing is perfect.*

There are many accounts in the Scripture where the Lord seemed to be late or to take too long. He stops to speak to a woman who received healing by touching his garment while on his way to heal a dying 12-year-old girl (see Mark 5). He wept over the death of a man He could have healed—only to resurrect him later (see John 11). Jesus slept on the boat while a storm raged, and his disciples panicked (see Mark 4). The urgency we feel is not shared by God. He feels no fear or anxiety. He is aware of all things.

Whenever He chooses a particular timeline, it is right. There are miracles that would not have been revealed in the Scripture if God had moved sooner or when people wanted Him to. Maybe you can think of a few of those instances in your life.

When God fulfills a promise in your life, don't be surprised if He asks for it back.

Abraham experienced this when God asked him to sacrifice Isaac (Genesis 22). What God was really asking Abraham to do was to murder his son. This story has never become common to me. One of the ways I tend to study the Scripture is to try to place myself in the shoes of the person who is being spoken of in a particular passage. It helps it to come alive and turn the Bible from faraway storybook to current and applicable Word of God.

> **GOD STANDS OUTSIDE OF TIME, AND HIS TIMING IS PERFECT.**

How would I respond to a request so impossible? A good father simply could not bring harm to their own child—especially not one they waited until their old age to have. The faith Abraham displayed was supernatural. The Bible says that when he was told by God to sacrifice his son, he got up early the next morning to do so.

It makes me ask myself, when God asks me to do something that is large in my eyes, am I prompt? Because obedience is not just about doing the thing. It is also about how swiftly you start and complete the task. Swiftness indicates trust. I respond quickly to that which is dependable, reliable, and consistent. I hesitate in situations of uncertainty, insufficiency, and lack.

When I trust the one who makes a request of me, I not only want to respond in obedience quickly but completely. Abraham prepared to sacrifice his son, as he would any other sacrifice. He brought the required materials and went to the correct place. He brought his son with him. When his son inquired about the sacrifice, he told him that God would provide one. Abraham did not say that because he knew the future. He said that because he had faith.

God did provide another sacrifice. Abraham had a dagger raised over his son's body, prepared to kill him, when the angel of the Lord called out to him to stop. There was a ram stuck in a bush nearby that he would ultimately use for the sacrifice. God already had the answer arranged; He was just allowing Abraham to go through the process of passing the test.

Abraham could have easily become frustrated with God when He asked him to sacrifice the son he had waited so long for. He could have been angry that the waiting was not enough and that even more was being asked of him. He could have resented the path God set, which was not linear.

Another example in the Bible is the story of Hannah bearing her son Samuel. She desired a son so deeply that she described herself as having a "sorrowful spirit" because she had not yet conceived (1 Samuel 1:15 NKJV). She vowed to the Lord that if He would give her a son, she would return her son to the Lord where he would remain all his days. When God granted her request and gave her Samuel, she kept her vow.

When we think about the things we want, are we willing to give those to the Lord if He grants our request? Or do we develop an entitlement if we have had to wait "too long" for the fulfillment of the promise? Do we see ourselves as the determiners of how long is enough? Or do we see God as the authority of time?

I remember making a vow to the Lord at 16 years old. I told Him that if He would deliver me from the season of lack I was in, I would spend the rest of my life serving others and helping them walk in the abundance that God has for His children. When I made that vow, the Lord did not respond by immediately delivering me. I could not see it at the time, but I needed to learn to wait on the Lord. This situation would prepare me for many others down the line.

Along my journey, I was presented with many shortcuts, schemes, and wrong ways to get myself out. I know it was the Lord who kept me from those options because I did not have the foresight to know how far-reaching the consequences would be. But I knew God, and I knew He had my best at heart. There had to be a purpose for the suffering. God would not have me in that place without good reason.

Many years later, the Lord reminded me of my vow when He brought me out of that season of lack. I was happy to keep my promise. It was a small way that I could show Him gratitude for His providence and goodness. Part of why He allowed the season of lack in my life was so I could minister to others from experience. I was not speaking from hearsay or from witnessing it happening to others. I could tell my story as the testimony that God can deliver them too.

Having that experience made me more effective in the roles and jobs I would eventually hold. He developed in me compassion, understanding, and grace, but also accountability, boundaries, and discernment. Having to face myself for years in a very authentic way meant He could use me to help others do the same.

He used the time that I was in the trial to break me of entitlement. He shattered my idea that God only works in perfectly straight lines, neat and free of any clutter. I learned that God was not someone I could calculate or pack into a formula I created that reflected how I thought things should work.

Sometimes, I envision certain life situations like I am at the starting line of a race. We expect the announcer to say, "On your mark(s), get set, go!" all at once. We do not expect them to yell out the first command and then leave the runners at the starting line waiting for 15 months. But our heavenly Father can see the whole racetrack. He made it. He can see the surroundings, the environment currently and in the future. He can see what is happening inside our bodies before we take off running.

It may feel at times like we just want to get going. We want to be busy doing something, anything so that we feel like progress is being made. Some of the sweetest times with the Lord, though, are those spans in between. If we just commune with Him, He will show us more of His beautiful heart and draw us closer to Him.

So, wait on the Lord. He will never guide us in the wrong direction. He will tell us the right time to go.

—On His mark, not mine.

JOURNAL DAY 12

1.   What time can I recount where I initially felt God was late, but, in hindsight, I can now see that His timing was perfect?

2.   What gift has God given me that He asked of me in a later season?

Devotional Day 13:

THE TWO WILL DO

²⁶ They came back to Moses and Aaron and the whole Israelite community at Kadesh in the Desert of Paran. There they reported to them and to the whole assembly and showed them the fruit of the land. ²⁷ They gave Moses this account: "We went into the land to which you sent us, and it does flow with milk and honey! Here is its fruit. ²⁸ But the people who live there are powerful, and the cities are fortified and very large. We even saw descendants of Anak there. ²⁹ The Amalekites live in the Negev; the Hittites, Jebusites and Amorites live in the hill country; and the Canaanites live near the sea and along the Jordan."

³⁰ Then Caleb silenced the people before Moses and said, "We should go up and take possession of the land, for we can certainly do it."

³¹ But the men who had gone up with him said, "We can't attack those people; they are stronger than we are." ³² And they spread among the Israelites a bad report about the land they had explored. They said, "The land we explored devours those living in it. All the people we saw there are of great size. ³³ We saw the Nephilim there (the descendants of Anak come from the Nephilim). We seemed like grasshoppers in our own eyes, and we looked the same to them" (NIV).

Moses sent spies into the land that generations before God promised to Abraham. There were 12 sent in total to investigate the people, the land, and the structure of the town.

When they returned, they reported to Moses, Aaron, and the people. They confirmed it was the land flowing with milk and honey, but went on to describe how strong and sizable the people there were. Then they made a statement much like those made for centuries, "We seemed like grasshoppers in our own eyes, and we looked the same to them."

The Enemy is so deceptive. God had promised the people the land, and He is so much bigger than any giant or any land or anything. Yet they allowed the image they had of themselves to supersede the promise of God. It is critical that we see ourselves the way God sees us. This is evident in the account of the spies' report of the land of Canaan. The spies returned and said they saw themselves as grasshoppers, and so did the giants in the land. But they had no idea how they were viewed by those who were in the land. They were spies, which means they were likely undetectable. They projected their idea of themselves onto others and accepted a defeat in a battle that was already fixed in their favor.

When the people heard the report, they rebelled. There were only two of the 12 spies, Joshua and Caleb, who delivered a good report. This was their account:

⁶Joshua son of Nun and Caleb son of Jephunneh, who were among those who had explored the land, tore their clothes ⁷ and said to the entire Israelite assembly, "The land we passed through and explored is exceedingly good. ⁸ If the Lord is pleased with us, he will lead us into that land, a land flowing with milk and honey, and will give it to us. ⁹ Only do not rebel against the Lord. And do not be afraid of the people of the land, because we will devour them. Their protection is gone, but the Lord is with us. Do not be afraid of them" (Numbers 14:6–9 NIV).

Even though their report is the one that fell in line with what the Lord had said, the people received the report made by the other 10 spies.

We must be careful whose report we believe and whose words we accept. We must also be careful what reports we give. Often, when God calls us, we will be alone or in the minority. He is looking for those who will serve Him, even when there are few who will stand alongside.

I remember learning a valuable lesson about being careful of what reports to receive and which to rebuke. I occasionally attended a small church where I hoped to experience spiritual growth and be discipled by the pastors there. At first, the church leadership appeared to be inviting and kind. The façade quickly faded, and I noticed things that were not of the Lord.

One evening at a virtual Bible study, there was a call for prayer. I raised my hand, thinking that they would pair me with one person with whom I could discuss my request. Instead, the pastor's wife and a group of other leaders in the church all were in the same virtual room with me. They did not ask why I wanted prayer.

> **WE MUST BE CAREFUL WHOSE REPORT WE BELIEVE AND WHOSE WORDS WE ACCEPT.**

The pastor's wife began to make declarations that I had the spirit of fear and the spirit of rejection. Others joined in making similar claims that they would need to "cast out" those spirits.

This is not a laughing matter, but I was holding back laughter like my life depended on it. This group had taken what little they heard about me from the pastor's wife and projected onto me how *they* would feel and what *they* would be suffering from if they had been in my shoes.

They wanted a reaction from me, but I gave them none. As they spoke, I simply filtered what they said through the Holy Spirit. He did not confirm what they said about me. I was grateful to know the Lord for myself so the lies the Enemy was using them to spew would not move me. But I was also saddened because I knew that if the leadership of this church community would do this to me, then they had also done the same to someone else. I could see how someone would accept the things the church leadership said as truth because of the position they held.

I was the only person in the room who had a different report. But I was comfortable standing alone because I knew I was not actually alone—He was with me.

Consecration and spending time with the Lord shows us His heart. By listening to His voice, our faith is strengthened so that our eyes can be transformed to see ourselves differently. Because I already knew that He called me more than a conqueror, head and not the tail, above only and not beneath, lender not borrower (see Deuteronomy 28:13), I could rebuke what was being said to me as a lie.

Equally important as knowing which reports to accept is knowing which reports to give. I remember being at the larger church I mention in the devotional on Day 5. The word the Lord gave me to speak, I knew would not be received well. Out of the large group of people on the worship team, there was only one other person who also had the boldness of God to speak the word God had given her.

I affectionately referred to us as the two spies—I still do. The worship team and the church leadership rejected us, but we maintained obedient to the direction of God. It was not easy. But God never failed to provide each of us with the strength we needed to continue.

We were only two against a large church institution. But the two will do when God has His hand on them.

When Joshua and Caleb gave the good report of the Promised Land, the people's response was that they wanted to stone them (see Numbers 14:10). But the Lord's response was this:

> *26 The Lord said to Moses and Aaron: 27 "How long will this wicked community grumble against me? I have heard the complaints of these grumbling Israelites. 28 So tell them, 'As surely as I live, declares the Lord, I will do to you the very thing I heard you say: 29 In this wilderness your bodies will fall—every one of you twenty years old or more who was counted in the census and who has grumbled against me. 30 Not one of you will enter the land I swore with uplifted hand to make your home, except Caleb son of Jephunneh and Joshua son of Nun'" (Numbers 14:26–30 NIV).*

Those who did not give the Lord's report would not enter the promise of the Lord. Further, there were grave consequences for spreading the bad report:

37 These men who were responsible for spreading the bad report about the land were struck down and died of a plague before the Lord. 38 Of the men who went to explore the land, only Joshua son of Nun and Caleb son of Jephunneh survived (Numbers 14:37–38, NIV).

Although the initial response from other people was unfavorable toward the two spies with the good report, they would later experience a much greater reward—entrance into the Promised Land. I saw a parallel to this in the story of my friend and me at the church. Our respective "Promised Lands" were those miracles, promises, and assignments the Lord had for each of us that were blocked until after we showed that we could be trusted not to go along with the majority. One of those assignments was the writing of this book. We were being tested to see if we would steward well what the Lord had for us. He has blessed us each in dividends that far outweigh the pain we experienced in the church. He fulfilled the word He gave in Romans 8:18: "Our present sufferings are not worth comparing with the glory that will be revealed in us" (NIV).

I will take a "well done" from my heavenly Father over the acceptance of other people every day of the week. I will both give and receive reports that only come from Him. For those who choose to prioritize the acceptance of man, we must pray. We ask God to open the eyes of those who are blinded and replace their words with His.

JOURNAL DAY 13

1. Search the word of God for what He calls His children so that you can discern which reports are and are not consistent with what He says.

2. Do I steward my own words carefully to avoid being a stumbling block to others?

THIS SEAT IS TAKEN

⁴ Samuel did what the Lord said. When he arrived at Bethlehem, the elders of the town trembled when they met him. They asked, "Do you come in peace?"

⁵ Samuel replied, "Yes, in peace; I have come to sacrifice to the Lord. Consecrate yourselves and come to the sacrifice with me." Then he consecrated Jesse and his sons and invited them to the sacrifice.

⁶ When they arrived, Samuel saw Eliab and thought, "Surely the Lord's anointed stands here before the Lord."

⁷ But the Lord said to Samuel, "Do not consider his appearance or his height, for I have rejected him. The Lord does not look at the things people look at. People look at the outward appearance, but the Lord looks at the heart."

⁸ Then Jesse called Abinadab and had him pass in front of Samuel. But Samuel said, "The Lord has not chosen this one either." ⁹ Jesse then had Shammah pass by, but Samuel said, "Nor has the Lord chosen this one." ¹⁰ Jesse had seven of his sons pass before Samuel, but Samuel said to him, "The Lord has not chosen these." ¹¹ So he asked Jesse, "Are these all the sons you have?"

"There is still the youngest," Jesse answered. "He is tending the sheep."

Samuel said, "Send for him; we will not sit down until he arrives."

¹² So he sent for him and had him brought in. He was glowing with health and had a fine appearance and handsome features.

Then the Lord said, "Rise and anoint him; this is the one."

¹³ So Samuel took the horn of oil and anointed him in the presence of his brothers, and from that day on the Spirit of the Lord came powerfully upon David. Samuel then went to Ramah (NIV).

Samuel had anointed Saul king of Israel, but later the Lord rejected him. There needed to be a new king. God again sent Samuel to anoint the next king, this time at Jesse's house. One by one, Jesse's sons came before Samuel. The Lord did not confirm any of them as king. Samuel then asked Jesse if all of his sons were present. Jesse responded by referring to David as "the youngest," who was tending the sheep. Samuel instructed Jesse to call for him, and David was chosen, anointed, and the Spirit of the Lord came upon him.

This passage of Scripture contains themes of the rejection of man, the favor of God, the sanctity of God's timing, and the power of His plan.

Jesse knew that the Lord's anointed would be chosen from among his sons, but he did not think to have David present. When asked if he had any other sons, he did not refer to David by name—only by his place in the birth order. He did not acknowledge David the way he acknowledged his other sons. Children need the affirmation of their parents and are sensitive to differences in treatment by comparison to their siblings. Without the Lord to fill the gap, we can easily fall into negative coping mechanisms to help deal with the rejection of a parent.

David's earthly father may have rejected him, but his heavenly Father showed him great favor. Seven of Jesse's sons passed before Samuel while David was outside working. God could have arranged for Samuel to spot David as he was traveling through the field. He could have given Samuel David's name ahead of time and not even considered David's brothers. But God timed it in such a way to show that it does not matter how many go before, the one He chooses will receive what He has set aside for them. There is no opportunity we can miss if God has it reserved for us.

God reserved the seat of the king of Israel for David before Samuel even arrived at Jesse's house.

And though David did not immediately proceed to sit in that seat, it was sufficient that God anointed him. The seat could not be taken away.

David did not make his own way to the throne. God chose him while he was working in a role that, on the surface, did not appear to be "kingly." He was to take care of the sheep, and he was obedient in that role, which meant he had a heart God could use. I love the clause in 1 Samuel 16:13 (NIV): "From that day on the Spirit of the Lord came powerfully upon David."

God did not just assign David the role of king and leave him. The Spirit of the Lord remained with David for the rest of his life. God offers us the same communion with His Holy Spirit. He will walk with us all the days of our journey if we accept Him.

I had an interest in owning rental real estate when I was a teenager, but no real knowledge of how to be a landlord. Fast forward years later to one day at work. I was sitting at my desk praying because I was desperate for God's guidance on a matter. As He often does with me, He spoke to me in that moment about something that seemed unrelated.

As I was pleading with Him internally, He said, almost suddenly, "Time to buy an apartment building."

I looked around momentarily, startled. Then I said, "Okay."

I still had little more knowledge than I did when my interest in real estate and rental properties started as a teenager. While I had no expertise, I was available. I did an internet search and called the first name I saw.

The person who answered the phone was polite enough, but sounded hesitant as he asked me questions. He asked who my investor was, if I had any partners, and if I was doing this alone. I was the investor. I had no partners. And I was doing this alone (in the natural, at least). He asked if I had prior experience. I had purchased my own home a few years before, but not a rental property.

He probably just barely showed up to our appointment that day, half expecting I was wasting his time. His demeanor changed as our showings progressed. I visited a list of buildings until I came to the last one; *the one*. I prayed as I walked through and knew this was what God had assigned to me.

The Lord provided all the right people to help with the process. He gave me assurances along the way that He was in control of the situation and that I did not have to let my inexperience make me afraid.

There was a list of buildings I saw, but He held the one He wanted me to have just for me. Other people saw the building before me. There were other interested parties. There were those who had more money and more experience than I did. But it was mine, so it remained. Some people who may have meant well advised me against purchasing the building. They talked about how difficult it would be, and that it would be detrimental financially and stressful emotionally.

The thing about when God leads it is not necessarily that you have no trouble with it. But you can be confident He will walk through it with you and use His supernatural hand to arrange even the negative things in your favor.

He has done that for me.

I did not realize it at the time, but the All-Knowing God was answering my frantic prayer at my desk that day. He answered in a way I could not have anticipated because I don't have the perspective He has. He knew the way to meet my needs that would produce dividends and longevity. I was only asking for a temporary solution to an issue, but He knew how to solve it long-term. I could only see one piece of the puzzle, but He saw the whole picture.

God used this experience to cause me to be open to other ventures about which I would have otherwise been hesitant. When the Holy Spirit would guide me into a place that was new or scary, I would think about how He arranged that building for me. I remembered that if He leads me to a place, He will guide me through the process.

I have watched God move this way in the lives of those around me as well. The house that the family wanted was under contract with another buyer. The contract fell through on the day of closing. We picked it right up!

The promotion was needed with the employer who doesn't give those kinds of promotions. They gave it this time because promotion comes from the Lord.

The child the couple desired to have but the doctors said it was not possible to become pregnant. So, the Lord gave them two.

When we understand that our steps are ordered by the Lord (see Psalm 37:23), then we can escape the trap of anxiety or the urge to manipulate or bend situations in our own favor. We do not need to resort to self-promotion. We do not need to exploit others to get ahead. We need not feel any envy when someone else gets something that we want or when they arrive to a certain space ahead of us. We do not have to feel inadequate if we are inexperienced or unqualified.

> **IF HE LEADS ME TO A PLACE, HE WILL GUIDE ME THROUGH THE PROCESS.**

There is nothing my God can't do. And when He has decided that He has reserved a seat for you, it does not matter who arrives first, who has more knowledge, money, or resources, or who is more recognized and celebrated. They will have to move for you to take your seat.

JOURNAL DAY 14

1.   **Recount times when God held a space for you, even when others arrived first.**

2.   **In what areas can you increase your faith in God so that you no longer try to make your own way?**

3.   **We are at the end of week two of the Daniel Fast. How have you witnessed God move as you deny your flesh and yield to Him?**

Devotional Day 15:

YES, I'VE BEEN PRACTICING

45 David said to the Philistine, "You come against me with sword and spear and javelin, but I come against you in the name of the LORD Almighty, the God of the armies of Israel, whom you have defied. 46 This day the LORD will deliver you into my hands, and I'll strike you down and cut off your head. This very day I will give the carcasses of the Philistine army to the birds and the wild animals, and the whole world will know that there is a God in Israel. 47 All those gathered here will know that it is not by sword or spear that the LORD saves; for the battle is the LORD's, and he will give all of you into our hands."

48 As the Philistine moved closer to attack him, David ran quickly toward the battle line to meet him. 49 Reaching into his bag and taking out a stone, he slung it and struck the Philistine on the forehead. The stone sank into his forehead, and he fell face down on the ground.

50 So David triumphed over the Philistine with a sling and a stone; without a sword in his hand he struck down the Philistine and killed him.

51 David ran and stood over him. He took hold of the Philistine's sword and drew it from the sheath. After he killed him, he cut off his head with the sword.

When the Philistines saw that their hero was dead, they turned and ran (NIV).

They *ran.*

David, by the power of God, defeated one Philistine man, and, by doing so, defeated an entire army.

When we think through the story from David's defeat of Goliath backward, we see God's hand at every step. First is the weapon by which David defeated Goliath—a stone.

Goliath was well trained in battle. He had the benefit of his large size and weapons that would help make him more effective. David had some rocks and a slingshot. When Goliath saw what weapons David brought to the battle, he mocked him. But God used one of those stones to enable David to knock the giant down and then David used Goliath's own sword to cut off his head.

The tools God gives you are enough. It might be a small or simple thing in your hand, but when God places His hand on it, He makes it divinely adequate for the job.

What we see just before David's victory is David's proclamation of Who would be winning this battle on his behalf—the Lord. David did not pretend he was sufficient by himself. He achieved victory because this was overflow from the time he spent with the Victor. He could speak to an impossible opponent in confidence because he knew that the One who sent him was bigger than the giant.

You will defeat everything God sends you to conquer if He is with you.

When David volunteered to face Goliath, Saul was afraid for him. He even gave David his armor with which to fight. David was respectful; he tried it on. But when he saw that it did not fit, he took the armor off and picked out five smooth stones from the brook.

God can choose to win a battle through us in a way that others have not seen before.

See, David had been practicing. When the lion and the bear came to take the sheep that he was called to look after, he killed them and retrieved the lamb. This is why we should do as the Bible says and not despise the day of small beginnings (see Zechariah 4:10). God will use those small beginnings to build the kind of character in us that can support greater things to come.

> **GOD CAN CHOOSE TO WIN A BATTLE THROUGH US IN A WAY THAT OTHERS HAVE NOT SEEN BEFORE.**

God will develop you in private, so you are prepared for that which you encounter in public.

A tactic of the Adversary is to choose opponents for us that are specific to our areas of weakness, vulnerability, or fear. The choosing of Goliath by the Philistines to be their representative was intentional. He was referred to as the "champion." So, it follows that the Philistines felt very comfortable sending this giant into battle for them. He would intimidate their opponent and win the battle on behalf of their people single-handedly. Goliath made statements that indicated how confident he felt in his own abilities. He told the Israelites to send their representative out to fight him, and whoever won that fight, won the battle.

Conversely, the Israelites did not have the same confidence. They did not respond by sending out their own champion. They listened in fear as Goliath taunted. The sending of Goliath temporarily succeeded in subduing the Israelites. The Philistines were getting the response they likely wanted from the Israelites—fear. The One who was not scared though, was God.

God is not intimidated by the size of our opposition.

God was not surprised that the Philistines chose Goliath. He was not moved at all by the odds or the likelihood or the statistics. He *allowed* the enemy to send out their best opponent so that His power would be demonstrated on behalf of His people. The greater the magnitude of the opponent, the greater God's glory will be revealed.

David could have felt inadequate to stand against the giant. He could also have felt too prideful to obey his father's request to take food to his brothers on the battlefield. He had already been anointed king. He could have felt that it was beneath him to continue to serve others. But David was acting in the way we are advised to in Luke 16:10: if we can be trusted with small things, we can be trusted with much. But if we cannot be trusted with those small things, we will not be trusted with much.

We should seek to be obedient, not just in the great things, but in the small and mundane.

My sister is one of the most grateful people I know. I have a memory that I will hold in my heart for the rest of my life because it impacted me that much. As I was on my way to meet her to obey the Lord in delivering the check to pay her debt after my first Daniel fast, she called me. She was cheerful as she usually is and said she had a story to tell me.

Recently, she began teaching a fitness class as a substitute teacher. She excitedly told me that she had taught her first class and was supposed to be paid $15 for subbing. I could hear her becoming emotional as she said, "Jessie, guess how much they paid me?"

Since I heard tears of gratitude in her voice, I fully expected her to say $50 or $100—or at least $30 which would be double what she was supposed to be paid. She paused, took a deep breath, and said, "$20!"

I must have blinked 47 times in one second. I asked her to repeat herself to make sure I heard her correctly. She did. I had heard her correctly.

The truth of that moment washed over me, and I had to put my phone on mute as she told me about the class and her compensation. I wept. She was *so* grateful to be overpaid by $5.

She could have scoffed at the extra $5 because she could have viewed it as having little effect on the size of the debt she was working hard to eradicate. She could have been polite when she received it, quickly thought of it as a nice gesture, and moved on. But she was deeply grateful.

I believe God ordained that conversation with my little sister that day. (It was for me; it was for you.) God had already cultivated that grateful heart within her. So, He knew He could bless her with a larger amount and know that she would give Him all the glory. Someone who can appreciate $5 that much is someone who God can trust with abundance.

When I handed her the gift bag with the check in it, I first recalled our conversation we had while I was driving to her, just a few minutes prior. I told her, "Because you were so grateful for a little, this is why God can bless you with much." She has the kind of heart God can use to do things great and small in His Kingdom.

I cannot adequately explain the gratitude I witnessed on her face, heard in her voice, and watched in her body language when she opened the bag and pulled out the check. There just aren't words for it. God had that wonderful gift prepared especially and specifically for her. He simply passed it through my hand to get it to her. See, she had been practicing integrity and diligence. She had been practicing stewardship. She had been practicing gratitude. This was the exact right timing for her to receive His gift.

David could have let the pressure to live up to the expectations of the king cause him to be unsubmitted to the King of Kings. He did not defeat the giant because he was bigger than or stronger than the giant. He defeated the giant because he was willing to set himself apart and be with God.

There was no scenario in which David would not have been prepared for this assignment as long as he stayed near the Lord. God knew what David would need before he met Goliath, before he was anointed king, before the lion and the bear. The Lord told Jeremiah in Jeremiah 1:5 that He knew him before He formed him in his mother's womb. So, there is nothing that the One who formed you cannot equip you for.

Practice what God has assigned to you. More importantly, when He gives you the victory, ensure that to God be the glory.

1.   What skills or character traits has God been developing in you in private that He may use in your next season?

2.   Are there any examples where God equipped you far in advance—even though you were not aware of His activity at the time?

3.   What are some opportunities for you to show the Lord gratitude that you may have missed in the past?

POUR IT OUT

To the Chief Musician. Set to "Do Not Destroy." A Michtam of David when Saul sent men, and they watched the house in order to kill him.

¹ Deliver me from my enemies, O my God;

Defend me from those who rise up against me.

² Deliver me from the workers of iniquity,

And save me from bloodthirsty men.

³ For look, they lie in wait for my life;

The mighty gather against me,

Not for my transgression nor for my sin, O LORD.

⁴ They run and prepare themselves through no fault of mine.

Awake to help me, and behold!

⁵ You therefore, O LORD God of hosts, the God of Israel,

Awake to punish all the nations;

Do not be merciful to any wicked transgressors. Selah (NKJV).

After David killed Goliath, thereby defeating the Philistines, Saul, the king on whose behalf David fought, called David to him. Saul asked him who he was, and he told Saul that he was Jesse's son. The Bible says that David became close with Saul's son, Jonathan, and that Saul took David into his own home. David did what Saul asked of him, and Saul gave David authority over his servants and army.

Then, Saul witnessed something that he allowed to shift his heart concerning David. Women with tambourines danced and sang, "Saul has slain his thousands, and David his ten thousands" (1 Samuel 18:7 NKJV). Saul became angry and resented David because of the comparison that was made, and he changed from loving David to trying to kill him, tear him down, and trap him.

David was experiencing the rejection of another important leader in his life. This time, that leader did not just dismiss him, he wanted to kill him because he was jealous. Saul allowed his insecurity to overtake him and drive him to wickedness. David began to run from the man he used to serve.

During one time Saul sought to kill David, he sent men to watch for him so they could take his life. David wrote Psalm 59 as the result of the experience of being hunted to be killed. Throughout the Psalms, we witness how open David is with God. He tells the Lord his true feelings. He is transparent, vocal, and direct. He even says things some of us would be afraid to say. David was respectful, but his candor shows us that he believed something about God that we can benefit from knowing: *God is holy, but He is not fragile.*

GOD IS HOLY, BUT HE IS NOT FRAGILE.

David asked God to "awake to punish all the nations" (Psalm 59:5 NKJV). He was not kidding around. He did not just want God to protect and deliver him from his enemies. He also wanted his enemies punished. He wanted retribution. He asked God to have no mercy on those who did wrong. David said exactly and honestly how he felt while Saul was trying to kill him.

God is the Most High King. So, we should always approach Him reverently and deferentially. But He does not require coddling or maneuvering. Nothing is taboo for God. He knows my innermost thoughts. I might as well be honest with Him about them. If I don't tell God and express my feelings to Him, I could be creating a weak spot for the Enemy to exploit. I may be swayed into coping with my feelings in maladaptive, or even sinful, ways.

An area that took me a long time to be able to talk with the Lord about is how I feel when I am in situations that were created as the result of my own unwise actions. I felt comfortable "telling on" other people who wronged me to God. But what about when it was my fault? I felt that if I had listened to God in the first place, I would not be in the current situation.

And that's true. But I have learned to come to the Lord in repentance and be honest with Him even in that space. That keeps me from expressing those feelings in a self-harming manner. I remember being deeply hurt by a friend of mine who God told me needed to be removed from my life. The Lord let me know that where He was about to take me, that friend could not come. I couldn't imagine my life without this friend. I did not understand why they had to go.

Then that friend of mine started to show their true colors. The behavior was ugly, manipulative, and just plain mean. I was devastated. This was a person I had trusted for years. Of course, the Lord knew that was coming. I nearly fell into damaging and sinful coping mechanisms because I was too ashamed to talk to God about it.

One day, during my devotional time, I was going through my prayer list topic by topic. The Holy Spirit whispered to me, "You know you can talk to me about that too." My eyes welled up with tears. I was so ashamed to have not listened to Him sooner. I could have saved myself so much heartbreak! But I finally was transparent with Him about how I felt. When I repented, He forgave me and healed my heart miraculously. He made me whole.

That began my journey of transparency with the Lord. I talk with Him about things I cannot tell my closest friends. When I am tempted to sin, I tell Him. I tell Him about my desires that don't align with His. I tell Him when I feel things are unfair.

When I was being mistreated by the pastor and leadership of the church where I served, I remember saying out loud to the Lord with a friend present the truth of how I felt. The wrongdoing was so blatant, and I felt unprotected and exhausted. So, I said to God, "I don't care what happens to these people at that church! It's not my problem! Now, I'm the one being obedient. Why do I have to deal with this?"

Actually, I'm pretty sure I yelled those words—I was at my wits end. I was tired of watching them get away with defying God and harming His people. I was sick of the lies being told about me, and I was fed up with the façade they presented to the congregation.

Then I paused. I took a deep breath in and out. Now that I had expressed my frustration, I felt ease enter my heart. So, then I said, "But I trust You. So, I will do whatever You ask me to do. There is nothing You can ask of me that is too much."

He gave me Scriptures that confirmed that I was on the right path and walking in His will. He reminded me of the privilege that it is to suffer when it is for His glory, found in 1 Peter 4:12–19:

> *[12] Dear friends, do not be surprised at the fiery ordeal that has come on you to test you, as though something strange were happening to you. [13] But rejoice inasmuch as you participate in the sufferings of Christ, so that you may be overjoyed when his glory is revealed. [14] If you are insulted because of the name of Christ, you are blessed, for the Spirit of glory and of God rests on you. [15] If you suffer, it should not be as a murderer or thief or any other kind of criminal, or even as a meddler. [16] However, if you suffer as a Christian, do not be ashamed, but praise God that you bear that name. [17] For it is time for judgment to begin with God's household; and if it begins with us, what will the outcome be for those who do not obey the gospel of God? [18] And,*

"If it is hard for the righteous to be saved,

what will become of the ungodly and the sinner?"

[19] So then, those who suffer according to God's will should commit themselves to their faithful Creator and continue to do good (NIV).

The Lord *chose* me to endure that trial. That passage was a reminder that when we are within God's will, we don't even suffer the same way we would in the world. It was never His intention for that trial to defeat me. He next took me to 2 Corinthians 4:8–9:

[8] We are hard-pressed on every side, yet not crushed; we are perplexed, but not in despair; [9] persecuted, but not forsaken; struck down, but not destroyed.

I was going to experience pressure; but that pressure was not going to succeed. He also reminded me that the suffering was temporary. He took me to Psalm 30:5: "Weeping may endure for a night, But joy comes in the morning" (NKJV).

God did not condemn me when I was honest with Him. He did not chastise me for having the feelings that I had. He was happy that I came to Him about it. And He gave me His Word to stand on so that I could outlast the trial. That conversation with the Lord was a pivotal point for me. The trial went on around me, but it was no longer within me. I felt complete and total peace about it from that moment on—no matter how I was being treated.

Think about how you feel when your children, or spouse, or friend, or employee comes to you and trusts you with an issue they are having. Their willingness to share with you indicates the depth of the relationship and their confidence in you. Even in our interpersonal relationships, we would be hurt if we found out that a family member or a friend turned to something that was harmful instead of reaching out to us. When we love people, we *want* to be supportive to them. How much more must God want to be there for us when He loves us infinitely?

David trusted God was bigger than his feelings. He was assured that God would not be moved by what moved him. He is a steady God, a Firm Foundation, the Dependable One. And He loves when we trust Him to be who He says He is.

So, be like David. Pour it out. He is a Great Big God. He can handle it.

1.   What topics have you been embarrassed or fearful to talk with the Holy Spirit about?

2.   In what areas can you ask the Lord to help you overcome shame so that you remove the Enemy's access in those areas?

3.   What maladaptive coping behaviors have you developed that you would like the Lord to help you remove from your life and replace with Himself?

SO HE STAYED TWO MORE DAYS

¹ Now a man named Lazarus was sick. He was from Bethany, the village of Mary and her sister Martha. ² (This Mary, whose brother Lazarus now lay sick, was the same one who poured perfume on the Lord and wiped his feet with her hair.) ³ So the sisters sent word to Jesus, "Lord, the one you love is sick."

⁴ When he heard this, Jesus said, "This sickness will not end in death. No, it is for God's glory so that God's Son may be glorified through it." ⁵ Now Jesus loved Martha and her sister and Lazarus. ⁶ So when he heard that Lazarus was sick, he stayed where he was two more days, ⁷ and then he said to his disciples, "Let us go back to Judea."

⁸ "But Rabbi," they said, "a short while ago the Jews there tried to stone you, and yet you are going back?"

⁹ Jesus answered, "Are there not twelve hours of daylight? Anyone who walks in the daytime will not stumble, for they see by this world's light. ¹⁰ It is when a person walks at night that they stumble, for they have no light."

¹¹ After he had said this, he went on to tell them, "Our friend Lazarus has fallen asleep; but I am going there to wake him up."

¹² His disciples replied, "Lord, if he sleeps, he will get better." ¹³ Jesus had been speaking of his death, but his disciples thought he meant natural sleep.

¹⁴ So then he told them plainly, "Lazarus is dead, ¹⁵ and for your sake I am glad I was not there, so that you may believe. But let us go to him."

¹⁶ Then Thomas (also known as Didymus) said to the rest of the disciples, "Let us also go, that we may die with him" (NIV).

Mary and Martha, in an attempt to save their brother Lazarus's life, sent word to Jesus who was a distance away, so that He might come to heal Lazarus of his sickness. Jesus made a definitive statement that Lazarus's illness would not end in death. Just a few verses later, Jesus tells his disciples that Lazarus is dead.

When Mary and Martha sent word to Jesus about their brother, they referred to him as the one Jesus loved. The Scriptures confirm this in John 11:5. It says that Jesus not only loved Lazarus, but Mary and Martha as well. Then it says something interesting. It says Jesus loved Martha, Mary, and Lazarus *so* He stayed where He was another two days.

This text is rich with the heart of God, even in the word choice. If we do not take a deeper look, we may think the Word is contradicting itself. It is not. When Jesus says that Lazarus's illness would not end in death, He is not lying, even though Lazarus does actually die. The word "end" is an important distinction. Lazarus did have to experience death, but it didn't end there.

The next portion that can, on the surface, appear to be contradictory is the fact that the Scriptures confirm that Jesus loved Mary, Martha, and Lazarus, but He did not come when they called Him, *on purpose*. Jesus knew Lazarus was going to die. He could have come and healed him. That's what Lazarus's sisters wanted. But Jesus intentionally stayed where He was for two more days. The operative word in this portion of the text is "so." Jesus loved them *so* He stayed where He was.

When Jesus did decide to go to Lazarus, His disciples were afraid because the Jews had wanted to stone Him there. Jesus was going anyway. He did not stay where He was for fear of being stoned. He told His disciples that He was glad they were not there so that they would believe. He stayed back so that He could perform the miracle of resurrection. The disciples had witnessed Jesus heal people. Those were wonderful miracles necessary for the growth of both those being healed and the witnesses. But now there needed to be a different level of miracle, to stretch the faith of those who witnessed, showing them that Jesus' power was not limited to the living. He had power over death too.

So many times, I have felt that God could step in and solve an issue I was having right then, but He did not. During one season, I happened to be studying the story of Lazarus—right before I would need to apply in my life the lessons I learned from that study. I was in a highly demanding job that had high visibility and was under great scrutiny. My job responsibilities included ensuring that the project was completed within the parameters of the policy, rules, and the law and that the integrity of the people and processes were intact.

But I noticed some things were not adding up. Documents weren't matching what I remembered seeing originally. There were secret conversations, inappropriate requests, and mishandling of funds. I suspected that one individual assigned to the project was being used to coordinate the wrongdoing, so I confronted her about it. There was proof of the wrongdoing that was occurring. I knew the other team members were using her so that if she got caught, they could feign innocence.

She was someone who claimed to be my friend. My job and reputation would have been in jeopardy if I did not do something about what I suspected. I asked her directly if she had committed the actions of which I suspected. Looking directly in my face, she denied it. She swore. It *offended* her that I asked. She said she would never put me in that position because she was my friend. She even produced real tears.

She was lying.

I asked her one more time to please tell me the truth. She profusely denied it. I told her I would have to show leadership the material I had proving otherwise, and I told her I was sorry that she would not tell the truth.

When she realized I was going to report the documents I had proving what I suspected, she finally admitted it. She said that she was being coerced into doing those things by her leadership. She said they were her friends and that they would not let her go down for these actions. I let her know they were not her friends; they would gladly let her take the fall.

She was given another chance after that. She continued the same behaviors that she was being asked to commit. When I found out the wrongdoing had continued, I was required to report it. This time, she was fired. She was fired, but none of the people who told her to do these things were affected at all. It was just as I had warned her.

The work environment became exceedingly toxic following her removal. People could figure out that I must have been the one to report it. There were passive aggressive threats being made toward me, bullying, and harassment. The people pretended to care that our coworker was fired, but the real issue was that the wrongdoing that was benefiting them so much had to stop. They no longer had a fall person to do it for them.

It would have been easy for me to simply be removed from that project and the group associated with it and placed on another one. There were procedures in place to do it. A person could be on one project on Friday and be moved to a different one by Monday. I asked God to do that. He didn't. I kept asking. He still didn't.

I felt nauseous every day I came to work. I was not afraid of the people, but the toxicity was wearing on me. I had done the right thing. I did what was both morally right and what was required of me in my job description. Why was I being punished for this?

As I studied the story of Lazarus's resurrection, the Holy Spirit began to reveal some things to me. I had to stay there in that job for a time. He had shown me how He can pull me out of a situation quickly. I already knew God, The Rescuer. But I needed to know God, The Sustainer. I needed to experience what Psalm 46:1 calls, "A very present help in trouble" (NKJV). I needed spiritual endurance and faith that was not only strong but long-lasting.

Sometimes, He leaves us in difficult situations on purpose.

So, I stayed. I endured while coworkers continued to mistreat me, and my leadership did not have the courage to support me. I watched while those who were ultimately responsible for the acts "got away with it." Some were even promoted to higher positions. My supervisors, who should have been covering me, participated in sabotaging my career progression so they could please others.

But when the Lord fixed it, He *fixed* it. He fixed it completely and made it right on my behalf. He elevated me and caused accountability to come to some of those who spoke against me. He placed me in a significantly better position. I was eventually promoted as well despite their best efforts to prevent that from happening. He entrusted me in the next season with greater responsibility because my faith and character had been developed to the point where He could trust me.

> **SOMETIMES, HE LEAVES US IN DIFFICULT SITUATIONS ON PURPOSE.**

My initial preference would have been for Him to just get me out of there. Mary and Martha's initial preference was that Jesus would heal their brother so that he would not have to die.

I cannot adequately describe how grateful I am now that the Lord did not just pull me out. I needed to know this other side of God—this other method of deliverance. I needed to know this part of my own character and faith—that, if I lean on the Lord, I can be sustained through great tribulation.

Jesus loved Mary, Martha, and Lazarus, *so* He stayed two more days. He loves me, so He left me in that job several more months. He wants us to be the best version of ourselves. He wants us to know that He is limitless and able to sustain us through anything. Know that in those "too long" seasons, He has not left you alone. He is right there and available to hear your cry.

JOURNAL DAY 17

1. In what uncomfortable seasons has God "left you" for what felt like too long?

2. What character or faith development was He accomplishing in you during that season?

3. What did you learn about God, His character, and His ability as you waited?

Devotional Day 18:

IT MUST LIVE

32 When Mary reached the place where Jesus was and saw him, she fell at his feet and said, "Lord, if you had been here, my brother would not have died."

33 When Jesus saw her weeping, and the Jews who had come along with her also weeping, he was deeply moved in spirit and troubled. 34 "Where have you laid him?" he asked.

"Come and see, Lord," they replied.

35 Jesus wept.

36 Then the Jews said, "See how he loved him!"

37 But some of them said, "Could not he who opened the eyes of the blind man have kept this man from dying?"

38 Jesus, once more deeply moved, came to the tomb. It was a cave with a stone laid across the entrance. 39 "Take away the stone," he said.

"But, Lord," said Martha, the sister of the dead man, "by this time there is a bad odor, for he has been there four days."

40 Then Jesus said, "Did I not tell you that if you believe, you will see the glory of God?"

41 So they took away the stone. Then Jesus looked up and said, "Father, I thank you that you have heard me. 42 I knew that you always hear me, but I said this for the benefit of the people standing here, that they may believe that you sent me."

43 When he had said this, Jesus called in a loud voice, "Lazarus, come out!" 44 The dead man came out, his hands and feet wrapped with strips of linen, and a cloth around his face.

Jesus said to them, "Take off the grave clothes and let him go" (NIV).

When Jesus arrived at the place where Lazarus was, Lazarus had been dead and buried in the tomb for four days. Martha went to meet Jesus, as He arrived, and told Him that if He would have come, Lazarus would not have died. She also expressed that she knew God the Father would still give Jesus whatever He asked.

Jesus then told Martha that Lazarus would "rise again," to which she responded that she was aware Lazarus would rise again "in the resurrection at the last day" (John 11:23–24 NIV). Jesus asked her if she believed in Him as the resurrection, the life, the Messiah, and the Son of God. She responded that she believed these things.

Martha called Mary to let her know that Jesus was there. Mary went to Jesus, crying, and telling Him that if He would have come, Lazarus would not have died. Her grief moved Jesus. When He went and saw where Lazarus was laid, the Bible says He wept (John 11:35). Onlookers questioned that the One who could restore sight to the blind could have also stopped Lazarus from dying.

Martha protested when Jesus asked the stone to be moved away from the tomb where they buried Lazarus. She feared that the odor from his decaying body would be offensive. Jesus reminded her of the importance of believing in God and called upon His Father to hear Him as He always did and show Himself strong to the witnesses there. Then He called loudly and boldly for Lazarus to come out of the tomb. To complete the resurrection miracle, Jesus had the people take off Lazarus's grave clothes.

There is no dead thing that can stay dead if the Living God says it must live.

> # THERE IS NO DEAD THING THAT CAN STAY DEAD IF THE LIVING GOD SAYS IT MUST LIVE.

When Jesus called out to the Father, He made a beautiful declaration in John 11:42: "I knew that you always hear me" (NIV). He was convinced and assured that when He called out to His heavenly Father, He was always heard. He wanted the witnesses that surrounded Him that day to become assured of the same thing and that Jesus was the Son of God.

Jesus exhibited the kind of faith that gives God something to respond to. It is significant that when He called Lazarus out, He did so in a loud voice. That indicated confidence and conviction that God is who He says He is and will do what He says He will do.

It can be scary to make faith statements when other people can hear them. It is one thing to hope for something quietly in your own heart. It is another to declare what the Lord has said in front of a witness. This is even more difficult in situations where the odds look impossible. But God can use our faith and testimony to draw people to Himself. When He gives us a word and tells us to speak it, we should be obedient in it.

Years ago, I had an epiphany about my first house that I was living in at the time. While I was extremely grateful for the gift that it was, the size of it was proving to be overwhelming as my level or responsibility was growing. I could not maintain the property to the standard I had held for years.

I decided I would rent out the house and move to a smaller place. I put the house up for rent—expecting to have some time to research my next place to live while it was on the rental market. It rented almost immediately. I had to move, and I had no place to go. Around the corner from my house, I found a condo for rent. The landlord was so kind as to let me in on very short notice. I signed a year lease.

It was my preference to own something, but I did not have enough time to find the appropriate property to purchase before moving. I did call the landlord several weeks into my lease, offering to buy the place I was renting if he wanted to sell it. He said he would think about it, but never responded to say he would or would not sell it.

One day, I was visiting a friend of mine at her house when I began to admire the details of her home. I love historic properties. There is a character and charm that cannot be replicated in new homes. I thought to myself, *I would love to own a place like this*. I imagined a version of her house that was a small condo, where I could have all the benefits of living in a historic property but none of the exterior maintenance responsibilities—aside from paying HOA fees. I wanted high ceilings, big windows, and original wood floors. I shook my head to shake the thought away because it was not possible.

Or was it?

The next day at work, I felt the Holy Spirit direct me to do a search for historic condos in my city. I thought, there will be plenty of historic *houses*, but no *condos*. I was obedient, just to see. A beautiful, late-1800s condo appeared on my screen. It had 12-foot ceilings, big windows, and original wood floors. I couldn't believe it, and I loved it immediately. The Holy Spirit directed me to a realtor, and we went to see it.

When we opened the door, we both knew that it was perfect for me. It was exactly what was in my mind when I first thought about it. Then the barriers began to float into my mind one by one. The price of the property was prohibitive. I was only three to four months into a one-year lease I could not break, and I would have to get rid of so many items to downsize into the space. It was a good idea, but it was a dead idea. I had just walked into the space of my dreams for no reason. I wondered why I could not have seen this property before I signed a lease.

Then I did something I had never done before—I decided to pray and give the whole thing to God. I would not interfere or try to "help." I said, "Lord, if this is my home, You will move all the barriers and turn things around in my favor." I sent the sellers an impossibly low offer, and I prayed that if He was going to give me the condo, the seller would respond with a counteroffer. If it was not for me, they would decline my offer altogether.

The sellers submitted a counteroffer, and I declared immediately that the condo was my new home. I began selling my things and preparing to move on that alone. I even declared to people in faith that it was mine. It still did not look promising, but I was determined to trust God completely this time.

He responded to that faith. He moved the sellers' hearts on the price, and He arranged for my lease to be taken over by someone who that property was perfect for. The individual bought from me all the furniture I could not bring with me to my new condo, so, I didn't even have to move them. We closed in time for me to spend my birthday in my new home.

And He even gave me the couch I wanted that suited the space beautifully. We serve a God that cares about a *couch*. He cared about that couch because it was the desire of my heart. And since I trusted Him completely, He completed the miracle on my behalf, down to the very last detail.

He had so many great plans related to me living in that condo. I appreciated the space functionally and aesthetically, but He had even greater plans and reasons for it. He could have arranged for a smooth transition into the condo that removed any of the obstacles I mentioned. But He needed me to know that He can revive the dead things. He can make the dead dreams and the impossible goals happen, and He can move the most immovable mountain.

When Jesus saw the grief of Mary and Martha and saw where Lazarus was laid, He wept—even though He knew He would resurrect Lazarus. He cares for us so much. He empathized with the people who were suffering and then He delivered them from it.

Trust the heart of the Lord. He is goodness and kindness and love. And if He says He will do something, He will do it—even if it requires Him to bring a dead thing back to life.

JOURNAL DAY 18

1.   Is there any area of your life that you have given up on, that you want to instead turn over to God?

2.   What faith statement has God called you to make that you have been afraid to declare?

Devotional Day 19:

NEVER TOO MUCH

John 12:1–11

¹ Six days before the Passover, Jesus came to Bethany, where Lazarus lived, whom Jesus had raised from the dead. ² Here a dinner was given in Jesus' honor. Martha served, while Lazarus was among those reclining at the table with him. ³ Then Mary took about a pint of pure nard, an expensive perfume; she poured it on Jesus' feet and wiped his feet with her hair. And the house was filled with the fragrance of the perfume.

⁴ But one of his disciples, Judas Iscariot, who was later to betray him, objected, ⁵ "Why wasn't this perfume sold and the money given to the poor? It was worth a year's wages." ⁶ He did not say this because he cared about the poor but because he was a thief; as keeper of the money bag, he used to help himself to what was put into it.

⁷ "Leave her alone," Jesus replied. "It was intended that she should save this perfume for the day of my burial. ⁸ You will always have the poor among you, but you will not always have me."

⁹ Meanwhile a large crowd of Jews found out that Jesus was there and came, not only because of him but also to see Lazarus, whom he had raised from the dead. ¹⁰ So the chief priests made plans to kill Lazarus as well, ¹¹ for on account of him many of the Jews were going over to Jesus and believing in him (NIV).

The Mary who anointed Jesus in this passage is the same Mary whose brother Lazarus Jesus raised from the dead. Mary took a bottle that was worth a whole year's pay and poured it on Jesus' feet. This was an extravagant offering that was used to prepare Jesus for the burial following the crucifixion.

When John writes chapter 11, he is intentional in placing this clause in verse 2: "This Mary, whose brother Lazarus now lay sick, was the same one who poured perfume on the Lord and wiped his feet with her hair." It follows that this extravagant offering reflects Mary's gratitude for giving her brother his life back. She also must have had so many things hidden in her heart for which to be grateful to Jesus, and she expressed that in the anointing of Jesus.

A natural response when we think of all that God has been to us and has done for us is profuse and expressive gratitude. It is an eager and cheerful generosity. It is swift and complete obedience. When the Lord asks something of us, a grateful heart responds with delight that He asked.

He gave us His all, so nothing He asks of us should be too much.

When I was days away from the deadline for completing this book and sending the manuscript to the publisher, the Lord asked something of me. The church I attend is states away from home. I attend once a month, and I get there by plane because I absolutely do not enjoy long-distance driving and avoid it at all costs.

I received an email on a Friday that my church was having revival that Sunday. I dismissed the thought of attending from my mind. After all, I had a book to finish that the Lord had assigned to me. Also, if I was going to get there in time, I would have to drive. That was not something I ever thought I would do to get there. I had appointments all day Saturday so I would not be able to sleep before driving.

I could not sleep that Friday night. The thought about attending revival would not leave me alone. But it didn't make sense. How was I going to finish the book if I drove that long?

It would not leave me alone on Saturday either. The Holy Spirit was asking me to go. I packed my car and started driving at 7:12 pm Saturday. I pulled into my church's parking lot at 6:57 Sunday morning.

On Monday, a friend of mine contacted me to ask how the revival was. It was wonderful. She knew I was working diligently on the book and how much it took for me to get to church. She reminded me that obedience is better than sacrifice and talked with me about a song she had been listening to that applied to that message. The lyrics spoke of the holiness and righteousness of God and how because of that, we cannot bring to Him things that we do not need or that cost us nothing. It described the heart of one who desired to give only that which was of the highest price and the very best that could be offered.

> **HE GAVE US HIS ALL, SO NOTHING HE ASKS OF US SHOULD BE TOO MUCH.**

The magnitude of the sacrifice ought to be worthy of the honor that is due our Savior. I looked for a Scripture reference as I listened to her describe the song, and I found 2 Samuel 24:24. It says:

But the king replied to Araunah, "No, I insist on paying you for it. I will not sacrifice to the Lord my God burnt offerings that cost me nothing."

So David bought the threshing floor and the oxen and paid fifty shekels of silver for them (NIV).

This confirmed to me that I should not only be *willing* to offer God that which is costly to me, but that it should also be my goal to offer Him the weighty, pricey things. It cost me something to drive all that way overnight with so much on my plate already, just to attend revival. And it should have. Is He worthy? He absolutely is. And He gave me so much during that time that I did not even know I needed—because He is faithful.

When we obey God and show Him appreciation in extravagant ways, that can be challenging to others—especially those who have not yet yielded to the Lord in that way. When Judas witnessed Mary's offering, he was critical of what she was doing. He said that the perfume should have instead been sold and given to the poor because of its value. However, his motives were impure. He was a thief who would steal from the money that was collected for which he was responsible, and he also was the one who would betray Jesus. Jesus correctly responded to leave Mary alone because she was doing the right thing.

We cannot allow other people's opinions to cause us to diminish our expression of admiration of the King.

We see an example of this in 2 Samuel chapter 6, in an account of King David. David was grateful for the blessing of the Lord that accompanied the ark that was being carried into his city. David began to dance before the Lord in worship. Saul's daughter, Michal, saw this and the Bible says she "despised him in her heart" (2 Samuel 6:16 NIV). David gave burnt offerings and sacrifices to the Lord and returned home.

When David arrived at home, he was met with Michal, who said, "How the king of Israel has distinguished himself today, going around half-naked in full view of the slave girls of his servants as any vulgar fellow would!" (2 Samuel 6:20 NIV).

Here was David's response:

> *21 David said to Michal, "It was before the LORD, who chose me rather than your father or anyone from his house when he appointed me ruler over the LORD's people Israel—I will celebrate before the LORD. 22 I will become even more undignified than this, and I will be humiliated in my own eyes. But by these slave girls you spoke of, I will be held in honor."*
>
> *23 And Michal daughter of Saul had no children to the day of her death (vv. 21–23).*

David was grateful to God. So, he did not allow Michal's criticisms to alter or affect his expression of worship.

I had an experience where my expression of worship was criticized. A pastor told me I needed to "tone it down." He ridiculed the way I worshipped through song and said, "I *could* mock you; but I won't." He smirked and jeered—hoping to discourage me into altering and minimizing my worship. The Enemy was using him in an attempt to prevent the Holy Spirit communicating to His people through me in the leading of worship.

It didn't work. That pastor did not know what the Lord had done for me. He did not know how many times He spared my life, answered my prayers, intervened on behalf of someone I love, or had an encounter with a loved one who was far from Him so that He could save their life. He was not aware of all the dark seasons the Lord has seen me through, how many ways He made out of no way, or how many desires of my heart He had satisfied.

In the book of Luke, when Jesus was traveling and approaching the Mount of Olives, the people there began to praise God loudly. The Pharisees told Jesus to rebuke the people; but Jesus responded, "I tell you that if these should keep silent, the stones would immediately cry out" (Luke 19:40 NKJV). So I'm going to worship Him *out loud*. I will not stifle my expression of gratitude. I will not be belittled for loving Him back. And I will have no inanimate thing give God greater praise than I will as His child.

When people feel insufficient internally, they can sometimes become critical of those who do not share that insufficiency as a projection of their negative feelings. They want those surrounding them to shrink back so they do not have to rise to the occasion. Do not accept that report. Accept only what the Lord says. He may call you to worship by giving an extravagant amount in a financial offering. People may criticize you or call you unwise for that. He may call you to move somewhere, stay somewhere, take on a role, or give of yourself in ways that seem illogical. He may call you to allow tears to flow during a worship set. Worship is trusting His voice and doing it anyway. If He is pleased with your worship, that is what matters.

When you allow your mind to think on just *some* of what the Lord has done, you realize that it is never too much. It is never too much praise, never too much obedience, never too much worship, never too much admiration. He is worthy of it all.

JOURNAL DAY 19

1.   Have you ever been criticized for an area of obedience or an expression of admiration of the Lord?

2.   Ask the Lord to show you areas where you may have allowed other people's opinions to minimize your expression of worship. Then ask for His help to remove the effects of others' criticisms.

Devotional Day 20:

FIERY FURNACE FAITH

^{20} And he commanded certain mighty men of valor who were in his army to bind Shadrach, Meshach, and Abed-Nego, and cast them into the burning fiery furnace. ^{21} Then these men were bound in their coats, their trousers, their turbans, and their other garments, and were cast into the midst of the burning fiery furnace. ^{22} Therefore, because the king's command was urgent, and the furnace exceedingly hot, the flame of the fire killed those men who took up Shadrach, Meshach, and Abed-Nego. ^{23} And these three men, Shadrach, Meshach, and Abed-Nego, fell down bound into the midst of the burning fiery furnace.

^{24} Then King Nebuchadnezzar was astonished; and he rose in haste and spoke, saying to his counselors, "Did we not cast three men bound into the midst of the fire?"

They answered and said to the king, "True, O king."

^{25} "Look!" he answered, "I see four men loose, walking in the midst of the fire; and they are not hurt, and the form of the fourth is like the Son of God."

^{26} Then Nebuchadnezzar went near the mouth of the burning fiery furnace and spoke, saying, "Shadrach, Meshach, and Abed-Nego, servants of the Most High God, come out, and come here." Then Shadrach, Meshach, and Abed-Nego came from the midst of the fire. ^{27} And the satraps, administrators, governors, and the king's counselors gathered together, and they saw these men on whose bodies the fire had no power; the hair of their head was not singed nor were their garments affected, and the smell of fire was not on them.

^{28} Nebuchadnezzar spoke, saying, "Blessed be the God of Shadrach, Meshach, and Abed-Nego, who sent His Angel and delivered His servants who trusted in Him, and they have frustrated the king's word, and yielded their bodies, that they should not serve nor worship any god except their own God!" (NKJV).

The king of Babylon, Nebuchadnezzar, fashioned a golden image and commanded the people to bow down and worship it whenever they heard the indicative musical instruments being played. The consequence for disobedience to this order was to be thrown into a fiery furnace.

The king placed Daniel's three friends, Shadrach, Meshach, and Abed-Nego, over certain affairs in the land. Some Chaldeans reported these men to the king because, as Jews, they did not bow to the golden image that Nebuchadnezzar had created. They brought the three men before the king, and he asked them if it was true that they would not obey his order. He reminded them of the consequence of their disobedience and asked them, "Who is the god who will deliver you from my hands?" (Daniel 3:15 NKJV).

Their response indicated a deep and solidified trust in the one true God. The three men answered the king, "O Nebuchadnezzar, we have no need to answer you in this matter. If that is the case, our God whom we serve is able to deliver us from the burning fiery furnace, and He will deliver us from your hand, O king. But if not, let it be known to you, O king, that we do not serve your gods, nor will we worship the golden image which you have set up" (Daniel 3:16–18 NKJV).

There is a simple but profound phrase in this passage that has so impacted my faith in the Lord: "But if not."

He wants us to have faith that is rooted in Him, not the outcome of the situation.

If God is only faithful when He solves things the way that we want, then we do not truly see Him as faithful. The three men were willing to obey God, even though it may have cost them their lives in an excruciatingly painful way. Nebuchadnezzar was angered by this and commanded that the furnace be heated seven times hotter than normal. He had the three men thrown into the furnace, bound and with all their clothes on. The furnace was so hot that the men who threw in Shadrach, Meshach, and Abed-Nego died.

Then, the king was astonished to see not three, but four men in the furnace, unbound and walking around. He said the fourth man looked like the "Son of God" (Daniel 3:25 NKJV).

When the king called them out, they emerged from the furnace without a single singed hair and no smell of smoke on them at all. Then Nebuchadnezzar blessed the Lord, made a decree that the people were to worship the God of those three men, and promoted them in Babylon.

> **HE WANTS US TO HAVE FAITH THAT IS ROOTED IN HIM, NOT THE OUTCOME OF THE SITUATION.**

This situation ended favorably for Shadrach, Meshach, and Abed-Nego, but making the decision to be obedient in the face of consequences does not always turn out that way.

Years ago, I was attending a church where I was informed of a peculiar policy on tithing. I was not present the times it was announced during the service, but several congregants told me about it. The church would periodically offer a "90-day money-back guarantee" for funds given in tithe. The rule was that if a person tithes for three months and God did not provide for their needs, the church would refund 100 percent of their tithe.

I thought it was a joke. But I eventually obtained the actual document that stated this. Those interested in participating had to provide their contact information, the "start date" of their 90-day period, and sign the agreement. They were pledging to give a full tithe on record and to request any refunds of the tithe within 30 days of the end of the 90-day period.

I really tried to let it go, but it would not let me go.

The Holy Spirit led me to write a letter outlining concerns with this based in Scripture. In a way which flowed, He gave me the contents of the letter, and I knew it was Him. Knowing the letter would not be received well; I did not want to send it. Some other people who knew about the letter I was writing agreed with its contents, but were concerned about the consequences I would face for sending it. I was concerned too. But I knew that the Lord would cover me. The outcome may not be favorable, but I had the favor of the Lord all over me.

So, I wrote the letter. In it, I discussed the issues with offering this guarantee. The Tithe Challenge: 90-Day Money-Back Guarantee perpetuated at least 4 significant lies, rooted in the demonic spirit of pride:

1.   The lie that we as humans possess the wisdom and purity of heart to determine what our needs are and what it means for God to adequately meet them.

2.   The lie that we are powerful enough to place upon an Infinite God a finite box of time in which to accomplish what we want.

3.   The lie that we are permitted to be obedient to God with conditions, strings attached, and our own will mixed in with His.

4.   The lie that the church, instead of communicating effectively that which the Holy Spirit leads can set itself up as an idol and a backup plan to God.

It was uncomfortable stating those four points that plainly. I did not want to be considered a troublemaker or someone who was speaking against the church. I love the church and part of love is accountability. I had been given an assignment to expose a trick of the Enemy. So, I expounded upon each point.

First, we do not have the wisdom to define our own needs. We certainly do not know what they are better than God. Proverbs 14:12 says, "There is a way that seems right to a man, But its end is the way of death" (NKJV). Without the leading of the Holy Spirit, we can be convinced of something deep in our hearts and still be wrong. That leads to the second issue. If we are wrong about what we think our needs are, we will also be mistaken about how long God should take to meet them. There is so much development that occurs while waiting on the Lord. Offering to refund people the tithe within a certain time robs them of the opportunity to see the Lord work the miracle in *His* perfect timing.

The third point represents a lack of faith that is a direct contradiction to the faith exhibited by Shadrach, Meshach, and Abed-Nego. It is not truly obeying God by returning the tithe in faith if there is a method to have it returned. If we are going to be obedient, we ought to be obedient completely and without conditions. The money-back guarantee was a backup plan to a false version of obedience. It would be like if Abraham said yes to the Lord when He asked him to sacrifice Isaac, but brought with him his own animal as a back-up sacrifice. He would have gotten in the way of the Lord providing the ram in the bush.

The last point is that the church ought to be teaching about the All-Sufficient God. When we see Him correctly as that, we have no need to create backup plans or escape hatches. We can stand on the foundation of His dependability and obey Him with reckless abandon.

I had experienced the joy of being obedient to God in the area of tithing. I had benefited from the spiritual development that comes from trusting God and being a cheerful giver, not one who gives to receive. This guarantee was a manipulation, a mockery of the Scripture. God does not require our assistance to prop Him up. He keeps His own promises. He makes His own ways. He is adequate and sufficient in every way.

The letter was not received favorably. No changes were made. But the peace I had reflected the grace of God, not the response of man. If I had needed the recipients of the letter to respond a certain way in order for me to be obedient to God, I never would have sent the letter. I trust that He used it for His purpose, even though I never saw what that purpose was.

Fiery furnace faith is a faith that says, "I know who God is. I trust Him even if He does not choose my favored outcome." It is the belief that God's choice, His movement, and His timing are always perfect.

1.   Ask the Holy Spirit to reveal to you any areas in your life where your faith is in the outcome, not in Him.

2.   What situations have you faced or are you currently facing that require you to obey God, even if it means severe consequences?

Devotional Day 21:

FREE INDEED

¹⁶ So the king gave the order, and they brought Daniel and threw him into the lions' den. The king said to Daniel, "May your God, whom you serve continually, rescue you!"

¹⁷ A stone was brought and placed over the mouth of the den, and the king sealed it with his own signet ring and with the rings of his nobles, so that Daniel's situation might not be changed. ¹⁸ Then the king returned to his palace and spent the night without eating and without any entertainment being brought to him. And he could not sleep.

¹⁹ At the first light of dawn, the king got up and hurried to the lions' den. ²⁰ When he came near the den, he called to Daniel in an anguished voice, "Daniel, servant of the living God, has your God, whom you serve continually, been able to rescue you from the lions?"

²¹ Daniel answered, "May the king live forever! ²² My God sent his angel, and he shut the mouths of the lions. They have not hurt me, because I was found innocent in his sight. Nor have I ever done any wrong before you, Your Majesty."

²³ The king was overjoyed and gave orders to lift Daniel out of the den. And when Daniel was lifted from the den, no wound was found on him, because he had trusted in his God (NIV).

King Darius appointed Daniel as one of the three administrators over 120 appointed governors or rulers. Darius saw that Daniel was of excellent character and wanted to promote him to being over the entire kingdom. When the administrators and rulers found out about this, they looked for something of which to accuse Daniel. They could not find anything, and they realized the only way they would be able to successfully accuse him is if the accusation had to do with God.

The administrators and rulers went to Darius and suggested he make a written rule that for the next 30 days, the people were to pray to no one but him. They would throw anyone who disobeyed into the lions' den. The king took their suggestion.

Daniel received the written decree but did not heed it. He still knelt down and prayed to God three times a day. The rulers reported this to the king. Darius was troubled because he did not want Daniel to be harmed. But the rulers were insistent that the king uphold the written decree he had made, so Darius ordered Daniel to be thrown into the lions' den. The king told Daniel that his desire was that Daniel's God would save him.

The den was closed with a stone and sealed by the king's ring. This is significant because it meant that no person could intervene to save Daniel. If deliverance were to come to Daniel, it would have to be by the hand of the God he risked everything to obey. What a perfect setup for God to do what only He could do.

The king was troubled all night long, while Daniel was in the den. At dawn, the king rushed over to the den and called out to Daniel, asking him if God had saved him. Daniel responded that God had shut the lions' mouths, and he was not harmed. This brought the king joy. They released Daniel from the den, and the king had the rulers who plotted against Daniel and their families thrown into the lions' den.

Then King Darius joyfully made a decree that everyone in the land must revere the God of Daniel. The Lord had delivered Daniel, even though there was an entire group of rulers who had plotted and schemed against him out of jealousy of the favor Daniel had on his life.

Daniel faced a critical choice, much like his three friends, Shadrach, Meshach, and Abed-Nego, when they were commanded to worship the golden image set up by King Nebuchadnezzar: obey God or lose your life. Those are drastic terms. When we read about something that happened so long ago, it can unknowingly turn into a fable or fairy tale in our minds. We would be wise to study the Scripture in such a way to be aware of the severity of its contents. In our contemporary context, we can sometimes miss the seriousness of these men's plights.

They must have already known in their hearts something that was written in the Bible much later in the New Testament in John 8:36: "Therefore if the Son makes you free, you shall be free indeed" (NKJV). When you know you are free in the Lord, you need not fear the consequences of following Him.

There is no safer place than in the center of God's will.

THERE IS NO SAFER PLACE THAN IN THE CENTER OF GOD'S WILL.

That is a statement we must know with absolute conviction. Daniel and his three friends already had practice choosing the ways of the Living God over the command of man. Daniel chapter 1 shows us how they chose to eat the way the Lord had instructed them over the way the king commanded. They set themselves apart then. So, when the fiery furnace and the lions' den came, they had already practiced using their faith muscle.

In all three scenarios, we see an earthly authority figure requiring something of them that went against what the Ultimate Authority had already said. In all three scenarios, we see that their obedience not only was a blessing to them but also served as a testament of the power of God that shifted the hearts of those who were requiring the opposing action in the first place.

These men served as an example of what it looks like to be free indeed.

So, let God do the work in you that He has planned. He wants to prepare you His way. He wants to use you as the vessel to draw more people to Him. He wants to purge you of those things that would harm you, others, and your witness.

As you end this fast, ask the Lord to help you remain sensitive to His voice and His leading. Ask Him to use His mighty hand to seal the heart work He is doing in you. Thank Him for His accessibility and His love.

For the past 21 days, you have been denying your flesh, communing with the Lord, and spending time in His presence. We serve a God of creativity and wonder. Any answer you are seeking, He has it. Any solution you need, He has already set up. Any wound you have, He has the salve. I pray that this is the first of many Daniel fasts for you. I pray that it becomes a regular part of your spiritual walk and that you meet Him more deeply every single time.

I pray that everything the Lord desires for your life, you are open to receive from Him.

JOURNAL DAY 21

1.   How has God either fulfilled or altered the answers you wrote to the questions listed in Journal Day 0?

2.   On this last day of the fast, document how God has spoken to you, changed your life or circumstance, answered a prayer, and shifted your heart.

Let's pray:

Lord, I thank You for the time You have spent with the person who is reading this book. I thank You for being a steady God—the One we can rely on for everything. Thank You for communing with us, for loving us, and for the sacrifice of Your Son on the cross. Great I Am, we adore You. We consecrate ourselves to You, now and forever. We hold these times of fasting as precious treasures in our hearts, and we place You as the King of our hearts. Please cleanse us and remove those things that are not like You. You are the Holy One. You are the Worthy God. And we give You honor for all that You are.

In Jesus' name, Amen.

ACKNOWLEDGMENTS

No one does a work like this alone, and God was so gracious to send my friends to complete this assignment. When the Holy Spirit first spoke to me about writing a book on the Daniel fast, my best friend, Akeim, confirmed it. **Akeim**, thank you for your no-nonsense approach to speaking the truth in love. You are a consistent voice in my life, my oldest friend, and someone I value immeasurably. God uses you so often to remind me of His infinite power and ability and His love for us.

To the other of the two spies at the Promised Land, **Chantel**, I thank you. You were my partner-in-faith when I was being persecuted. You had the courage to stand with me when so many others did not. And then you read the entire book, giving me invaluable feedback that aligned with God's whispers to me. You communicated what the Holy Spirit told you, and by doing so helped me stay in the center of His will. May God continue to use you in mighty ways and bless you richly.

Thank you so much to **Sarah Wronko** and the team at Clear Wind Publishing. I asked God for the right group to help me complete this work and distribute it. You came well recommended by my friend and writing accountability partner, Kim. I know God ordained this partnership, and He will get the glory for the fruit it produces.

Kim, you spoke into my life and provided solutions that I know were from the Lord. You had faith that this work would be completed. You taught me to celebrate. You checked in, not just on the progress of the writing but also on the state of my spirit and my heart. Thank you for your friendship and accountability.

Chef Keema, you came highly recommended by Kim, and I have had the benefit and privilege of experiencing why she so highly regards you. You delivered delicious recipes right on time. You shared your gift with me and the world in the way God has specifically gifted you to do. Thank you for your ideas, support, and understanding. I pray a blessing over your life.

Finally, to my sister, **Janelle**. You are my picture of what God's kindness really is. You're my little sister, but you protect me like none other but God. God knew to use you to start my journey with fasting. He knew that the beautiful heart He gave you would inspire me. I pray you always maintain your sweet spirit, your kind approach, and your willing generosity. You inspire me to be the best person in the Lord that I can be.

I appreciate you all more than I can express. Thank you.

Citations

[i] Joseph M. Scriven, "*What a Friend We Have in Jesus,*" 1855. Composer Charles C. Converse, 1868. Public Domain.